Chasing Chickens

RETHINKING CAREERS, RETHINKING ACADEMIA

Joseph Fruscione and Erin Bartram, *Series Editors*

CHASING CHICKENS

WHEN LIFE AFTER HIGHER EDUCATION DOESN'T GO THE WAY YOU PLANNED

RACHEL NEFF

University Press of Kansas

© 2019 by the University Press of Kansas
All rights reserved

Published by the University Press of Kansas (Lawrence, Kansas 66045), which was organized by the Kansas Board of Regents and is operated and funded by Emporia State University, Fort Hays State University, Kansas State University, Pittsburg State University, the University of Kansas, and Wichita State University.

Library of Congress Cataloging-in-Publication Data
Names: Neff, Rachel, author.
Title: Chasing chickens : when life after higher education doesn't go the way you planned / Rachel Neff.
Description: Lawrence, Kansas : University Press of Kansas, [2019] | Series: Rethinking careers, rethinking academia | Includes bibliographical references and index.
Identifiers: LCCN 2018058796
ISBN 9780700627936 (pbk. : alk. paper)
ISBN 9780700627943 (ebook)
Subjects: LCSH: College graduates—Vocational guidance. | Job hunting.
Classification: LCC HF5381 .N3653 2019 | DDC 650.14—dc23
LC record available at https://lccn.loc.gov/2018058796.

British Library Cataloguing-in-Publication Data is available.

Contents

Series Editors' Foreword   vii

Introduction: My Life App Crashed
after the Latest Update   1

1. How I Got into This Mess   11

2. I'm a Doctor. No, Not That Kind of Doctor.   17

3. Getting Over the Fear of "No"   45

4. Is It a Dragon or a Windmill?   65

5. Chasing Chickens (and Other Shit I Didn't Think
I'd Have to Do with a PhD)   89

6. The Best-Laid Plans of Mice and Control Groups   101

7. Sticking the Landing   113

Series Editors' Foreword

Welcome to Rethinking Careers, Rethinking Academia. Rachel Neff's *Chasing Chickens: When Life after Higher Education Doesn't Go the Way You Planned* marks the beginning of what we hope will be a robust and helpful series. We plan to provide much-needed resources to help readers understand how academia works, expand their career options, and develop their skills for a variety of fields. Rachel's is the first of the guidebooks we're creating for various career paths in, around, and outside academia.

Chasing Chickens shows how "rethinking" academia can—and, given the academic job market, *should*—start as early as graduate school. "I am not the same person who drove down with her father to [UC] Riverside in 2007," she writes in chapter 1. "I learned to navigate an office environment, classroom, and independent project. I was pushed and, in turn, pushed myself further than I imagined. Before I started, I had no idea what graduate school was really like or really about." As the inaugural book in our series, *Chasing Chickens* gives you the kinds of advice Rachel and many of us who did our graduate work in the late 1990s and early 2000s didn't get. It's a great book for someone at the beginning of a professional journey—whether that journey is into or out of academia. Rachel will bring you through her journey as she experienced it . . . but with the benefit of the knowledge she's gained since leaving academia.

You won't just be getting Rachel's story as a series of successes, inspirational decisions, and personal experiences. Instead, you'll get solid advice about balancing work and life in graduate school, as well as about rethinking one's academic skills, experiences, and aspirations. She smartly blends personal anecdotes with timely advice on figuring out graduate school and the alt-ac landscape. As she reminds us, "When you begin to frame conversations and opportunities as 'the worst that will happen is they say "no,"'" you begin to make things less about your fears and more about your possibilities. If 'no' is the worst that will happen, then it's worth the risk of hearing 'no.' Besides, if you don't try, you won't have the chance to succeed."

Here's hoping that reading about how some of Rachel's professional journey involved chasing chickens—literally *and* figuratively—helps you succeed in whatever way you need to. Whether you're picking up this book at the beginning of your PhD program, in the middle of some doubts about the academic path, or at the beginning of a new journey away from academia, we hope you'll be able to jump-start your own process of rethinking both your professional self and the path you're on.

Joseph Fruscione and Erin Bartram

Introduction

My Life App Crashed after the Latest Update

This wasn't the plan. This isn't supposed to be my life. After spending the majority of my twenties pursuing a degree I rarely use in a professional capacity, those two sentences run through my mind a lot. The perception of education in the United States, particularly for office-based work, is that following a prescribed course of study will result in automatic admission to a career. Similar to a math formula, the process appears to be "Study X, Become Y." When I studied Spanish to a doctoral level to be able to teach at a university, I thought I would become a professor. Study. Take exams. Apply for jobs. Get job. Graduate with PhD. Live a fabulous life of the mind. That did not happen. Not by a long shot. But it's not all bad. Keep reading.

The idea behind writing a book about what to do when the life you planned for isn't the one you end up living percolated for many years and went through several itera-tions. What started off as a list of things I wish I had known while I was a graduate student shifted into a memoir, then ended up a hybrid of a cautionary been-there-done-that tale meets this-will-all-be-funny-one-day advice book. I wanted to impart what I needed to hear most of all after I graduated. With no idea of what to do next, I faced a complete reevalu-ation of my life and the identity of who I thought I would be after I got my degree. Bereft and feeling alone, all I wanted to hear was how things were going to be okay.

But who am I to give words of wisdom on life after higher education? I was a high-achieving student who went from a 4.0 in high school to summa cum laude in college and then straight to graduate school. When I decided univer-sity teaching was my passion, I expected to spend my ca-reer being called "Doctor" or "Professor." My last year as a doctoral student was spent working on my dissertation and polishing job applications. The months passed by, and the academy's complete disinterest in my candidacy grew more apparent. When I started looking for help and advice, there was some "quit lit" of people who had left the academy, but most of the articles and books at the time were written by people who had been in adjunct positions for several years. Very little was available from people like me who never truly got a start in their profession.

During my final year as a doctoral student when my field's major professional conference came and went, I had to face an uncomfortable reality. No university had extended an interview invitation. All the papers I presented. All the conferences I organized. All the syllabi I created. All the times I prioritized a line on my CV instead of the people who I was with and the moments I was living. Without reaching the end goal of an academic job, the sacrifices were for nothing. I had worked for years for something that hadn't happened and was never going to happen. The entire future, my entire adult identity, centered on being bright and bookish. At every turn in my academic career, I had been one of the best. Honor roll. Outstanding student. Scholarships. Fellowships. Time and time again I had beaten the odds and come out on top.

When my idealized life as a professor did not materialize, I had to reevaluate my personal and occupational trajectories and start on reinventing myself. Being hardworking and smart wasn't enough. My best efforts and individual sacrifices weren't enough. This meant I felt like I wasn't enough. I experienced a mixture of sadness and anger. I spiraled into asking myself what more I could have done. I beat myself up for the subject matter expertise I chose. I second-guessed every decision I had made. I was the greatest failure.

Writing this book, I thought about my journey from graduate school to alternate academic career to the private sector. I tried to gather all the emotions and experiences behind those transitions and the mishaps along the way. I felt a sense of loss and grief. My well-ordered and carefully

planned existence had come to an abrupt change. By bring-
ing together my misadventures, false starts, and personal
failures, I wanted to show that perhaps what I went through
was similar to others who graduated from high school or
undergraduate studies and entered the workforce for the
first time. In an effort to help those who might feel as direc-
tionless as I did after studying for a professional career they
did not ultimately follow, I chronicled some of the stories
behind the lessons the world outside of the university taught
me.

What do I mean by lessons? It's one thing to say, "Don't
get comfortable in a job that doesn't value you." It's another
to personally experience a short-term contract where one's
assigned office is a room full of floor-to-ceiling, wall-to-wall
paperwork, a room for which one is forbidden to have a key.
I took away the lesson of not keeping more personal items
than I could carry in one trip when employed in precarious
contract-based situations. The next step was applying that
lesson. Because of my first, terrible contract position, I was
cautious about similar short-term work. So, a few years later
in a different contract job, I had an unexpected meeting with
Human Resources where I was laid off. I left the building
with the few personal effects I brought with me jammed into
my purse. Once outside, I called the state unemployment
department and watched another person struggle to carry a
box and huge peace lily as she cried and walked toward the
bus stop. I could look at her situation and say to myself, "At
least I didn't have to take a potted plant home on the bus."

What If You're Stuck with a (Metaphorical) Potted Plant?

I remember my hooding ceremony as a mixture of joy, pride, relief, and disappointment. In part, the turmoil stemmed from facing an uncertain future. Having gone from a well-defined career path to the complete unknown, the rest of the summer—the rest of my life—was a blank slate.

What can you do when the life you planned for doesn't go according to plan? For me, I was in the company of 66 percent of doctoral graduates—more than 35,600 a year—who, according to the National Science Foundation in 2011, would not find full-time, tenure-track jobs after graduation. The statistics helped me see that I was not alone. In fact, I was in the majority.

Whether you were premed and didn't get into medical school or earned a doctorate and didn't land a tenure-track job, you begin to wonder if all the work and sacrifice over the last several years were worth not reaching the life you imagined for yourself.

Perhaps your peer group and family don't understand why this transition is so difficult. Maybe they don't understand the stress and anxiety that can come alongside such a radical departure from a planned professional pathway. To them, your situation and reaction may not make sense. Perhaps you've even heard, "But it's just a job and not that big of a deal." Part of what might make this period of time more difficult is watching others strive for and achieve what you wanted. The gut-wrenching feeling of failure happens because you are confronting a reality that doesn't match your expectations. Jealousy and anger are common emotions. You get to grieve the life you dreamed about but never got to realize.

Nevertheless, even when facing a deeply uncertain future, it is important to recognize that life changes. It's okay to start your education thinking you want one thing and decide halfway through or at the end that you want something else. There are a lot of voices and opinions—and not all of them are nice—about folks who decide to step off, leave, or avoid the prescribed track altogether. It's easy to comment from the peanut gallery, but it's harder to be living and making the choices that will, at times, seem to alienate you from the community you have spent many, many years trying to become a part of.

Was the PhD Worth It?

I am so relieved, proud, and happy that I finished my doctorate, but many times I wished I had walked away with my master's and moved on. One classmate and I agreed that we were more certain about marriage than continuing on to a doctorate. My life would have turned out differently, both professionally and personally, but at the same time, by finishing my doctorate, I never have to wonder, "What if I had gotten my PhD?" Even in the worst of times, I turn back to the reality that if I had quit after two years, I would not have made the same friends and scholastic support network. I wouldn't toss away those connections and experiences to save myself from heartbreak and temporary disappointments.

Sure, I miss digging through archives and wandering about stacks and stacks of books. I wish my days were filled with mentoring students and watching them grow into more confident, polished individuals. However, I don't regret leaving the stress or the uncertainty of the academic job market. I left academia a lot sooner than most. I made the choices I did and the decisions to support them based on where I was at the time. I refuse to live my life looking in its rearview mirror.

As my graduate studies wound down, I found a community online. (If by the time you read this we're communicating via chips implanted in our neocortices, then go forth and find your folk there.) More and more, I discovered stories from and voices of people who experienced similar circumstances.

One of the common circumstances was learning to grow from mistakes and failures rather than successes. Moments of personal crisis have been few and far between, and yet I learned so much in those times of stress and despair that they form the majority of my recollections and advice. If my experience had been seamless, then I would not have as much advice to share with you now.

What's the Plan? Is There a Plan Here?

Understand the following. No matter what, you are not alone. The human experience is simultaneously unique and universal. Much like notes with harmonies, other stories will resonate with your own. That's what I hope, in part, my stories about falling down and getting back up will do for you.

The first step of life outside the academy is accepting that you're not ending up where you thought you would. Getting your life and not-quite-as-planned career in order means resetting your expectations and recovering from those feelings of disappointment and failure. It's not easy, but I've already been there, and you're going to laugh, cringe, and feel a lot better after reading this book.

Chapter 1 starts off explaining how I got myself into this mess and my history of failing at things. The next chapter is where I share what I most deeply regret about my time in graduate school and talk about what my first real attempt at finding full-time work outside of academia was like. In chapter 3, "Getting Over the Fear of 'No,'" I share how I got used to rejection and how to move forward despite your own feelings of inadequacy. Chapter 4 focuses on seeing the bigger picture and not getting lost in minutiae. In chapter 5, I will reveal the story of how I ended up chasing chickens on New Year's Eve as part of my job. The sixth chapter covers finding your next career and approaching interviews outside your field. Lastly, I talk about sticking the landing, no matter what happens.

In order to help take all the uncertainty and stress of re-inventing yourself and to focus the many different directions your mind might be taking you, I end each chapter with a series of questions to help put your current situation into perspective. The purpose of the questions is to start you on the process of self-reflection. These inquiries begin to prepare you to look outward at yourself, then help you look inward at your own stories, skills, and professional anxieties. Besides, at some point, you'll be able to look at what happened to me after I left behind the life I spent years planning, then look at what you're going through, and be able to say, "At least I didn't have to chase chickens."

1

How I Got into This Mess

Perhaps I should have taken some of the things that happened to me while interviewing at graduate programs for placement as signs that the pathway I was taking wasn't going to go quite to plan. While visiting the school in California I eventually attended, I decided to walk a few blocks from where I was staying to buy some aloe vera. (Fun sidenote—you can tell who moved to California by how sunburned they are in their driver's license photo.)

In the dark parking lot, a truck almost hit me. I did a polite, small-town wave of *It's no big deal*. The guy rolled down his window and said, "Get in the car. I've got money." At the time, my brain didn't fully comprehend what had just been said to me. Shaken, I ran inside.

On the second day of my visit, I had another unfortunate experience. While I was in my motel room, a man tried to break in. He started banging and pounding on the door. Then, he screamed a different woman's name saying that he had paid for his time and he was going to get it. The door wasn't the sturdiest, and the thin plate glass window wasn't much of a barrier. I yelled back at him to go away and that I didn't know who the woman was, but he kept trying to force open the door.

I panicked. Calling 911 wouldn't get me help in time if he got in. I grabbed the motel receipt and dialed the main number.

"Please, help," I sobbed. "There's a man trying to break into my room." The front desk receptionist raced around the corner to the back of the property.

"Get away from that door!" she yelled at him.

I heard a car door slam and tires screech. The guy fled in a white, windowless van (of course). The clerk moved me to a different room and comped me for the night. I also learned that dialing o from your room will connect you with the front desk. Not that any travel advice books have a section explaining what to do when someone tries to break in.

Still terrified, I dug through all my emails and found the department chair's phone number. Crying, I asked if he would pick me up and drive me the three blocks to campus the next morning. He did pick me up, and he made sure I had a ride home from campus.

Despite those two incidents during my campus visit, I still chose to attend. The people I met made the difference. The good news was that I did not experience any other major events while at that school.

The Summer before I Started Graduate School

Shortly before I left for California, I searched "graduate school horror stories" and discovered a webpage by a student who left her Spanish graduate program that told all the horrible things that happened. The writer made multiple indictments against the department. It did not instill me with confidence to pack up my life and move down to California. Having turned down a well-paying content writing job and still smitten with the idea of teaching college-level classes, I continued toward the path I thought I wanted to travel. I approached graduate school with a sense of fear and dread.

The biggest piece of advice I took from that blog post was to have a Plan B. When you have a Plan B, it is much more difficult for anyone—boss, supervisor, peer—to bully you. Your Plan B also lets you think about the world outside of the rhythm and routine of formal education. It is very difficult to talk about or openly discuss leaving or seeking a job outside of what you trained for, which for me was being a professor. The nicest backhanded compliment I received in graduate school was from one professor who was upset that I talked about wanting to work at a community college. "There are plenty of students to whom I would say that would be a fine career. But you, you are much better than that. You should be working at a research institution." Spoiler alert: I didn't end up as a professor at all.

Hindsight is the clearest phenomenon of your life. Looking back, you realize all the directions you could or should have taken, if only you knew then what you know now. Along with having a Plan B, another piece of advice I wish I carried with me when I started my postbaccalaureate journey was to cast a wide and ambitious net. If you are going to fail, then fail while reaching as far as you think you could possibly go. As far as my worldview goes, there is only one direction to go—forward and onward.

Meeting other budding scholars at conferences, I realized I could hold my own with my future peers from institutions with a prestigious pedigree. When I finished my undergraduate degree from my public university, I did not have the confidence to apply to a bigger, name-brand school. Even though I don't have an Ivy League degree, I'm incredibly grateful for the skills I learned and the depth of knowledge I gained.

In graduate school, I oscillated between being extremely cocky and completely insecure. Graduate school permitted me to hide from a crashing economy and pursue my love of learning. I watched friends enter the workforce only to be displaced a few months later. In the years since graduate school, I have experienced work insecurity, and that stress never really leaves you. To know that your future is precarious regardless of your hard work makes life outside of the academy much more stressful. There's a prevailing idea that education inoculates against economic downturns. The reality is that everything is precarious in our modern society.

Looking Back

Thinking back to graduate school, I don't know that I ever really reached my stride. I'm sure my peer group would disagree with that, since they all seemed to come to me for advice about one thing or another. What I do offer to folks is that you can get through life after academia in one piece. I'm confident because I worked hard and through sheer grit and determination at times, I completed a large, written work that formed the basis of my last three years of graduate school. It was a process that shaped me as a scholar and as an individual.

I am not the same person who drove down with her father to Riverside in 2007. I learned to navigate an office environment, classroom, and independent project. I was pushed and, in turn, pushed myself further than I imagined. Before I started, I had no idea what graduate school was really like or really about. It is a process of breaking you down, building you up, and then setting you loose on the world a better researcher, a more critical writer, and a future faculty member.

Now that I've talked about my not-so-perfect start and not-so-ideal finish, here are a few questions to begin the process of introspection as you plan your next steps.

- What is the first job you remember wanting to have as a child? How close or far away from it was what you ended up studying?
- How many people do you know personally who ended up doing exactly what they planned on?
- Who are three people you know outside of the academy who you could talk to about their career path?
- What are three things (people, movies, places, sensations) that bring you joy?

2

I'm a Doctor.
No, Not That Kind of Doctor.

The greatest regret I have from graduate school is not a
class I didn't take or a summer institute I didn't attend.
Rather, my greatest regret remains not visiting my paternal grandmother before she died. The last time I saw her
in person was the July before I started my graduate studies.
We hung out at her country home, where I learned her two
dozen laying hens produced one to two eggs a day, every
day. She loved her chickens. She had a quilted purse with a
giant rooster on it.

My great-grandmother lived to be ninety-eight. When
my grandmother died, she was in her mideighties. I always
thought I had more time. When I called her from Spain after
finishing my first year of doctoral studies, she thought being able to make a long-distance call for pennies per minute

was the neatest thing. I told her about all the chicken decorations I had seen on my weekend trip to Porto, Portugal. I promised to visit soon. I sent her a postcard.

Time in graduate school passed quickly. Before I realized it, I was in my fourth year, preparing to take my postponed doctoral exams. Swamped with preparing to sit my doctoral exams, I had forgotten to mail my grandmother a birthday card. Instead, I called. We chatted at length. She shared so many memories—almost missing the last bus with her girlfriends in college, her joy at being a kindergarten teacher, how ever since I was a young girl I always had to do things my own way. I planned to visit her in late July, after I finished teaching a summer course. I told her I was taking my qualifying exams in a month, and promised her I was going to finish my PhD. We made plans for me to come out and visit that August when I finished teaching summer school.

It was a visit I would never make.

The second-to-last week teaching that summer introductory Spanish course, I woke up feeling strange. In part, the morning was unusual because I got up well before my alarm. There was a clarity to the moment of consciousness. The world felt off. Out of kilter.

The phone rang. It was my father, calling to tell me my grandmother had had a stroke. I asked if I should fly out immediately. He said there wasn't any need to leave my responsibilities. What my father didn't tell me at the time was that she was already mostly gone. She died with my father holding her hand. It was a few days after the Fourth of July, just two weeks before I was supposed to go visit her for the summer. Rather than flying to see her, to catch up, to spend time, I boarded a flight to bury her.

There is never more time. There is the moment you are living in. You will never get it back. The perception that the academy or your employer demands everything and all from you in order for you to be successful is flawed. We don't get to go back in the past and relive things. Don't pass up something because you feel things are too busy. Evaluate your priorities and make time for the things that really matter. Don't live with the regret of what you should have done with the people who matter the most to you.

Remember, life moves forward. Do not let other people dictate your priorities. The only loyalty you owe is to yourself and the people you love. A job can replace you. Another student can take your seat. Live your own life. A company will not value loyalty. It will value the bottom line. Breaking yourself into a million pieces for someone else isn't worth it. You don't get to go back in time and redo things.

I share my greatest regret not for pity, but rather to illustrate how life changes in a matter of hours. The plan was to visit in a few weeks. The reality became I flew out for her funeral. Although we had talked on the phone and exchanged correspondence, I allowed graduate school and the pursuit of tenure-track employment to overshadow all my other life priorities.

Grief mixed with regret is a toxic brew. It took years to forgive myself for not spending more time with her. How quickly the time had passed. The rage at how little I had noticed.

However, my stubborn streak kept me going. Even when I wanted to give up and go off and be all but dissertation (ABD) for the rest of my life, I remembered the promise I made that final phone call with my grandmother—that I was going to finish and graduate. I remembered how she said she was so proud of me for pursuing my PhD. Because I made a promise to someone who really mattered, and even when I wanted to quit, I didn't want to let her memory down. I dedicated my finished dissertation to her with "sorry you left before I finished."

While there is a delicate balance between pushing toward a new intellectual frontier and burning out, whatever you work toward should not become so all-consuming that you lose sight of life's bigger priorities. The most miserable year of my life was not because of what I was striving for, but rather what I forgot to hold dear while doing so.

My Grandmother's Death Was Difficult Because I Forgot My Boundaries

My early twenties had started out more promising. Having nearly burned out after finishing my baccalaureate, I put boundaries in place to better balance my work and life. I made a list of three things I would not give up.

No matter what you're about to embark on, make a list of three things you will absolutely not give up. This is good for jobs, relationships, and any kind of pursuit in life. I know, making a list may seem silly, but the purpose and act of writing down what is most important to you is very serious. By writing down and thinking about what you hold most dear, you are setting up a boundary. Boundaries are extremely important to both getting through your day-to-day and to navigating the expectations of and external stresses from others.

When you write down the three things you will not give up for anything, you are telling yourself these things are most important to you, and whatever you're about to pursue is not worth losing them. Make this list. Make boundaries. Mean them.

The year before my grandmother died had been extremely difficult for me, personally and professionally. I realized I had given up too many of my initial limits. I wasn't sleeping very well. I had lost touch with what was most important to me, and I had let preparing for my qualifying exams and writing my first dissertation chapter take over my entire life.

What had gone on? I almost ended a six-year long-distance relationship because I felt I couldn't spare a weekend to visit. I missed my favorite aunt's wedding because I felt in that moment I couldn't spare any time to fly out and attend. What was most upsetting about the decisions I made was that I missed out on a lot of family events, and I still ended up taking an extra year to finish my dissertation.

Things Had to Change

When I realized my passions were all-consuming in a negative way, I set about reestablishing my boundaries. I thought back to the summer after high school when I volunteered for the YWCA. Toward the end of my time there, I trained on how to answer a crisis hotline. Although I never put what I learned into practice, one of the key takeaways from the training has stuck with me over the years—put your own oxygen mask on first. The trainer's sage advice was that you couldn't be there for anyone else if you weren't looking after yourself first and foremost. In fact, if you didn't go and secure your own mask first, you were useless. Once your own oxygen mask was secured, then you could help other people. This mask is figurative, and it represents whatever you need to be successful, unstressed, and balanced both emotionally and physically.

So you have to learn that you do not need to carry the weight of the world on your shoulders. When individuals work at a high intellectual capacity, they often experience a lot of pressure internally and externally to produce near-perfect work. In fact, many who continue on to graduate studies often produce finished projects that they consider mediocre but that others consider high quality. There also are misperceptions about high-achieving individuals. One common one is that they don't make mistakes. Another is that they enter the workforce ready to go without instructions. Frequently, they may be tasked with more projects and to-dos than they can reasonably accomplish in a work week.

Academics in general and high achievers in particular seem to thrive on working at all times of the day rather than renegotiating expectations, saying "no," or seeking help to reduce the workload. While setting clear boundaries may feel as though you are breaking an invisible cultural rule of never saying "no" to work, what is more likely to happen is that you are able to better negotiate the demands of your professional life with how much it does (or does not) encroach on your personal time.

The responsibilities of others are not your problem, nor are they things you need to take on alone. Give people resources, but protect your time and emotional energy. Someone else's lack of planning or foresight does not make it your emergency. You are responsible for your own success, and you are not responsible for the success or failure of others.

If you want to achieve your dreams and goals, you have to be selfish at times. You can't worry about pleasing everyone else. Part of learning to be selfish is figuring out when to ask for help and when to let go of things so someone else can step in and do them for you. Not taking care of yourself and letting external situations and influences dictate how you feel in your day-to-day life is going to leave you overwhelmed. Whether it's your dissertation supervisor or direct report at work, sometimes what is being asked of you is not possible to complete in the amount of time given. Learning how to negotiate and navigate expectations will make pushing back against unreasonable expectations easier.

The Breaking Point

I needed to go and put on my own oxygen mask. In doing so, I had to start confronting my deep perfectionism. Until my dissertation, my career had been on track. I did everything in order. I always aimed higher, worked harder, and put in more time than my peers. My work was rarely late. Unfortunately, I did not fully comprehend the amount of reading and research that needed to go into a dissertation. Flippantly, naively, I thought a dissertation would be just like a longer term paper. I did not appreciate the wealth of information and background I would need on the topic in order to begin to formulate a larger argument and in order to make sound and logical conclusions.

Asking to cancel my scheduled qualifying doctoral exam was a defeat. I held out as long as possible, engaging in magical thinking that another week or two would be enough time to make up preparation that was really months behind schedule. As the date of my exam loomed closer and closer, I knew I was in over my head.

The dissertation chapter I needed to complete as part of the qualifying exam process was not anywhere in good enough shape to go to a defense. If finishing a dissertation chapter weren't enough stress, I still had a significant number of works to read for the written portion of the exam. It was clear the process was not going well.

Sitting in my adviser's office, my ears rang and the world started becoming small when I said to him in this mewling voice, "I don't think I'll be ready to take my exams this year." I had spent so much time building up this idea that my adviser would be so incredibly disappointed in me for not taking these exams. I felt embarrassed and humiliated knowing other students who entered the program after me were further along with their research projects and writing.

Taking in small, shallow breaths, I tried not to start sobbing, even though I felt my eyes watering. I stared at the edge of my adviser's desk, not wanting to see if my fears were true. He very calmly and kindly said, "That's okay. We'll cancel your exams. You can let us know when you're ready to take them. I'd rather you have a better long paper and pass your qualifying exams than rush and be asked to take them again."

I looked up, slightly stunned. I had expected to be dressed down, to have to face a look of disgust or disappointment from my adviser—my academic idol. Instead, I was fortunate enough to have a compassionate and caring individual who was sincerely concerned for my well-being.

Sometimes we allow our own perceptions of what others expect of us to hold too much weight. It is more often than not a negative perception based on our own unexamined fears rather than facts and reality. In the grand scheme of things, another year wasn't a big deal. Fortunately, I wasn't the first student to fall behind schedule. Once the relief washed over me, I was able to reset my own expectations of myself and my work.

Saying Goodbye

So, when my grandmother died a few months after I reached my breaking point, I was able to compartmentalize and handle my personal family matters. I briefly shared with my summer students that my grandmother had served as one of my inspirations for becoming a teacher, as she had been a kindergarten teacher for many, many years. They were very understanding and kind, even in the student evaluations. I graded their exams before catching my flight. Any delays in the trip to the Midwest would mean missing her viewing.

Despite some turbulence and the threat of thunderstorms to the east, my flight arrived on time. After my grandmother's viewing, my father and I went to her assisted living facility apartment. I saw the postcard I sent her from Spain on her refrigerator. Sitting on the edge of her empty bed, I was hit by the weight of the loss. Even though I had begun to reevaluate my priorities, I realized I would never smell her again. Never hug her again. I could live the rest of my life wallowing in that regret.

Instead, I hold on to that last visit. In particular, I return to the memory of my cousin flying my grandmother and me around the farm in his twin-engine plane. My grandmother grew up wanting to be like Amelia Earhart. Instead, she became a kindergarten teacher. The allure of the sky never left. The quick takeoff and landing—the way a hen darts about a coop—brought a smile to her face. Our last snapshot together was taken that evening. Her face glowed with joy at seeing the world below. I think of that trip above the farm, her childhood home, as our little chicken flight.

You're Probably Not Alone

Even though I had started to relieve some of the pressure on myself by postponing my doctoral exams, I still struggled for months with the guilt. One specific element that added to my sense of failure was the incredible weight of expectation I felt from my family, professors, and peers. All their hopes for me wrapped in well-meaning comments about where I was headed with my career and future. Every time I went off the prescribed path, I came down hard on myself. I felt I had not only failed myself, but I also had failed them. It's hard to accept a large change in your life because of how American culture worships youth. Lists of "30 under 30" and such make it hard to feel like a success when you are nearing or over thirty years old. Having to restart a career or life path after putting so much effort into one that didn't work out is incredibly heartrending. After experiencing a major change in life plans, it's easy to doubt your talent and ability. When the people around you are your only source of perspective, it's easy to feel like you're failing or drowning. It is much easier to be unkind to yourself based on how you fear others will judge you.

A friend of mine had gone to college with the dream of becoming a doctor. In fact, she had spent high school getting as much premed knowledge as possible. We met in the honors/advanced placement (AP) track and have remained dear friends. As our undergrad graduation approached, she confided in me that not getting into medical school—her goal of more than a decade—was one of the most emotionally devastating events in her life. Her premed degree focus served as a constant reminder of those aspirations. As I struggled to finish my doctorate, we spoke over the phone. She reflected back on that time in her life and how rough things were before graduation, watching friends and classmates announce acceptances to medical school after medical school. Then, she said she woke up one day and realized, "I'm okay with not being a doctor."

Sometimes, we don't realize how valuable a conversation is until years later. One of life's greatest slaps is when doing all we could either isn't enough or doesn't matter. Facing a similar professional identity crisis, I remembered our chat.

My friend's life was filled with joy. Although I sensed she felt a bit of longing to attend medical school a few years after finishing her bachelor's, the further she journeyed through her life, the less she regretted how things turned out.

"Do you think I'm a failure?" she asked one day while I moped about my future.

I thought she was a success. She had a job she loved in a field she had studied. She was happily married and had a wonderful life. In no way did I feel medical school defined her worth. Then her comment that she felt okay with not being a doctor clicked for me. If she could look back on the past five years and be fine about how her life turned out, then maybe I too could be okay with not being a professor.

Part of the process was accepting that I went down a path for my life that I was no longer going to follow. While finishing my dissertation, I had spent a term as an adjunct professor. But after spending a morning waiting in the pouring-down rain because I was not worthy of a building key, I swore the $2.50 an hour I was making between grading, class prep, and travel wasn't worth it. My labor had market value and, by gar, I was going to find something that paid decent wages with benefits.

What about the Original Plan of Being a Professor?

Think of the original plan you made for your life as a pair of pretty shoes. You buy them, take them out of the box, but then you have to walk in them. Sometimes shoes fit flawlessly, and they are like a second skin. Sometimes you put on a pair of shoes, walk in them a bit, and your feet are blistered, sore, and bleeding. This metaphor is to explain that it's okay if one pathway doesn't work for you.

No one thinks badly of you if you never wear a pair of shoes again, right? The same thing goes for the profession you thought you would have after you finished your course of study. If you decide a certain career or job is not for you, it is absolutely okay to walk away, quit, or stop. You are not a bad person if you decide this. You are not, nor will you ever be, a failure if you decide to leave. Everyone outside the academy will ask, "So, what are you doing now?" It isn't a big deal.

At every point in my graduate school career, I had choices to make. Frequently, the advice I was given was based on the job market of twenty years ago. While I appreciate the well-meaning words, many of them were outdated or meant for a path I was no longer going to take.

Culturally, we get told if you work hard and make the right connections, the world will be your oyster. Finding your footing out in the real world can take some time. The narrative of college equals good job is not necessarily true anymore. Besides, there are amazing individuals who are brilliant colleagues who have their credentials from life. What is truly unfair is that many positions demand college degrees for skills that are not necessarily acquired through formal education.

Everyone thinks they will buck the trend and make it, even when they are told the odds are long or the chances are slim to none. I know I did. I had no idea how difficult the job market was or would be. I thought I did everything right, and when I went on the job market, I had no interviews for tenure-track or lecturer positions. Not a single one. I had a 4.0 in high school, a 3.91 in undergrad with a double major and double minor, and busted my ass in graduate school. I worked on committees, organized conferences, and did transatlantic research in the hopes of diversifying my job potential. I'm hoping my first (and for the time being, last) time on the job market and the complete lack of interest from any university was due to the fact that I only had two out of five dissertation chapters done by December 2012. When I defended my thesis, my adviser said, "I don't know why some people get job offers and others don't. You had a strong portfolio."

So many positions advertised wanted the ability to teach two separate Romance languages. In order to master those skills, I would have had to have been raised bilingual or gone to a bilingual school and have picked up a third language by the end of undergrad. More and more, the demands of the job market reflect the schism between those with the most access to education and those who use public institutions to gain a foothold in life. To add salt to the wound, many of these positions paid a pittance. The system wanted thousands of hours of mastery for a song.

Even the job advertisement language was a slap: "A successful candidate will . . ." Reading the requirements of the jobs was painful. At times, it seemed like the job ad should read, "A successful candidate will have a crystal ball and be known to have studied the three Romance languages our department wants." Other folks in the alternate academic (alt-ac) community regularly lambaste and lampoon these descriptions for what they are—a unicorn in a sea of work horses.

Perhaps if I had gone back on the job market the following year, I would have received more offers. But, you can't live life looking in the rearview mirror. I decided I wanted more than chasing tenure around the country. Every move would cost more money, and there was no guarantee I would pull myself out of the visiting professor or one-year lecturer track. Instead, I decided to find another line of work.

I'm okay with that decision. I don't regret it. I won't sit on the outside of the table of academia begging for scraps. I recognize a lot of this advice hinges on lots and lots of class and privilege. I received financial help from family and a partner after graduate school. My last year when I was underemployed and then unemployed, I did not have to worry about taking out more loans or paying for school or putting a roof over my head because they gave me money to cover all those expenses. At my lowest point in the ten-month-long job search, I looked at the box holding everything from my teaching assistant office and felt so defeated that I imagined myself writing "FAILED DREAMS" on the top in Sharpie and donating the entire contents to charity or throwing it all away.

The lines on my CV with the conferences I organized— they're fading away. Each new computer. Each batch of files uploaded. The details of the life I used to live become less and less important. Every year I move further away from the life of "Doctor" and "Professor." I cringe less when I am addressed as "Miss." I am slowly forgetting all the little things that mattered so much at the time. The paper topics. Class subjects. Teaching evaluations. The particulars of my day-to-day graduate school life no longer hold the stress, weight, or meaning they once did. They are still a part of what got me to where I am now, but their importance to my life has diminished.

All the things I once thought were so critical to my future success don't mean anything these days. None of that experience is pertinent to any of the jobs I apply to. Adding an extra year to my degree wasn't the end of the world. What's more, by putting my own oxygen mask on first and looking out for myself, I finally had a sense of peace about finishing. With the help of regular counseling, I felt I had a great weight lifted from my mind. Whatever I had imagined was worse than what had actually transpired. When I decided not to spend another year on the academic job market, I drew on that wisdom that the facing the unknown is worse than facing the fear.

Taking my beautiful, four-page CV and cutting it down to a résumé felt like a defeat. Everything I had worked on, everything I had poured hours of my life into were deleted. A job as a copy editor doesn't care how many conferences I organized. However, a position as an executive assistant might find that information enlightening. Stripping away all the details to the heart of what you offer is a key step to helping explain why you are a good fit for a gig.

Looking for work takes a lot of time and energy, particularly when you try to sell a skill set outside of your original field of study. You have to sell the brand of you. Who are you? First of all, you are not your job. A job title is packaging a bunch of activities together. Tell about the results. What did those activities *do*? What did you accomplish? Examine the activities and projects you participated in. Find ways to translate your knowledge and skills into the language of what the employer or client is looking for. Find something that makes you ask yourself, "What am I curious about today?"

As you decide your next steps given that what you were planning to do is no longer what you're doing (that's a mouthful, isn't it?), take some time to evaluate what matters most in your next move.

Starting to Look for a Job off the Tenure Track

When I decided to focus on a new career path, I knew I would have to position myself to an audience unfamiliar with what my degree and training meant for them. It took some practice, but I worked at sounding comfortable rather than bitter about my transition. In part, the bitterness lessens with time. But, most importantly, the feelings of anger that make you sound bitter soften over time. Holding on to those negative emotions really takes a toll. It is very difficult to go forward when you keep looking back at where you thought you would end up. No magic pill exists to make this easier.

Training and studying for a career I was no longer going to pursue made me feel as though I had wasted years of my life. At the time, the most painful part was not having anticipated a scenario where no one wanted to interview me. I went into my tenure-track job search with no geographic restrictions. I applied for all sorts of job opportunities, hoping to snag a last-minute lectureship or visiting professor position. One by one, the emails and letters came in: thank you for your consideration, you were not selected, the position has been filled. Such a conclusion was something I hadn't considered. Spring brought a harsh dose of reality for me. Starting a completely nonacademic job search was intimidating. I started applying to anything that moved.

So, when planning your next move, make a list and answer the following questions:

- Is geography important?
- Position?
- Salary?
- Will anything, any job do?

If geography is important—and by that I mean needing, wanting, or having to stay in a certain area or city—then concentrate your efforts into finding the best job that most suits you in that place. Use your network. Many jobs are never advertised. As you're looking, ask friends and family members in that industry if they know anyone who works at the place you're applying to. Sometimes, you have to send out a lot of résumés before you even hear a "no." My first foray into full-time employment took over five hundred applications across the United States.

When looking where you want to live, remember to weigh the cost of living. I moved from Texas to Oregon and the difference between what I could rent in the Southwest versus the Pacific Northwest for the same amount of money was notable. I used an online resource to calculate the difference in the cost of living. Armed with that information, I was better equipped to negotiate salary. I didn't want my geographical shift to result in slightly more money but less buying power.

I have finished interviews knowing I nailed them. After one interview, I felt that if I weren't offered the job it was because there was a better candidate. After another, I knew if no offer was extended it was because my salary requirements were too high. I was right on both occasions. Interview skills take time and practice. I have listened to interviewees go from top candidates to no longer considered because of how they answered questions.

Take the time to find common interview questions. Although it was published in 1989, *The Robert Half Way to Get Hired in Today's Job Market* has a lot of the common questions to expect during a job interview. There are several online sources of common job interview questions as well. Behavior-based questions are particularly popular. With that in mind, you want to have stories that illustrate your skills. Keep those stories brief and have clear and concise answers to the questions being asked. The standard format for these behavior-based questions is often, "Tell us a time when you used X to accomplish Y."

In one interview I participated in as an interviewer, we lobbed the standard "So, why are you leaving your current/most recent company?" at the interviewee. Our problem wasn't with the situation the interviewee described, which was of galling wage theft and labor abuse, but rather how this person told us the story. Instead of a quick "people were being pressured to lie about their hours so the company wouldn't have to pay overtime," we were told the entire situation in detail. The interview had turned into a therapy session and the interviewee was still bitter and angry.

Leaving a job you hate is difficult. So is starting a job search in a field you didn't originally plan on pursuing. You have to learn how to spin the experience. Keep it succinct. Remain positive. Have a one- or two-sentence answer. If pressed, be able to speak a bit more about the details, but don't focus on every little one. An interview is as much about how the company is a good fit for you as you are a good fit for the company.

If you have a bad feeling early on about a job being a poor fit, know that things won't likely get better. Trust that feeling. A job that sounds too perfect or too good to be true will more often than not show its flaws in short order. Ask hard questions of the company during the interview. See what the turnover rate is. Dig in to why the last person left or why they are creating this position. Most importantly, do not ignore signs of a troubled or unhappy workplace. Look online for employee reviews of what working there is like. Life is too short to work at a place where everyone is miserable.

The most important thing to keep in mind is that hiring takes time. Even when companies are in a rush to fill an opening, it is very rare that you walk into an interview and get hired on the spot. (Although that has happened to me.) Some companies do multiple rounds of interviews. Others take lots of time between gathering résumés and either sending rejections or extending interview invitations. No matter how qualified you are for the jobs you've applied to, it takes time and perseverance. Be prepared for the job applications to number in the hundreds.

Finding the Right First Job

Sometimes you read a job description, apply, and know that you are looking at your future job. I've applied to positions that would have made do, and then I've applied to jobs where I said, "That's mine." This was the case when I found the ad for the first nonacademic job after finishing my doctorate. I tailored my cover letter and résumé to the position by adding in keywords and select phrases from the posting. I remember when I was invited to do a two-hour test for the position.

I was really excited to move into another phase of the application process. However, I had started to play cello with the university orchestra as a way to stay busy, pass the time, and make connections on campus in the hopes that those interactions might lead to a job. It was the end of summer in Texas, and I didn't want to leave my cello in the car while doing this test. So, I asked if it would be a problem for me to bring my cello inside with me. Had the answer been "yes," I would have skipped rehearsal. Fortunately, the answer was "no," and I traipsed into the interview with my giant green cello case strapped to my back.

There is something to be said about making a first impression with a cello that makes you look like a misshapen turtle. In hindsight, I might have chosen to skip rehearsal anyway. For the record, it was a memorable entrance. Granted, I play an instrument so large that my parents often wondered out loud, "Why couldn't you play the piccolo?" Later, one of my coworkers said that he knew I was the person to hire because of the cello.

Before the test began, the interviewer asked me what I thought the biggest challenge I would face at the job would be. She laughed when I said, "Giving up my beloved Oxford comma." I also explained how my expert knowledge of Modern Language Association (MLA) style meant I could easily learn the rules from a new style manual. Remember, always translate the knowledge you already possess into concrete advantages and benefits for your future employer.

On a more serious note, I suspect the reason I got the job was because I was the only candidate who said I could do the test faster if I had known more about Associated Press (AP) style. My answer was sincere. The MLA style background I had meant that I knew what things to look for during the test. Of course, being a teacher for many, many years, I knew where good test questions might be based on different style guide requirements. As an unabashed word nerd, I knew that commas, numbers, and capitalizations were prime spots for diverging recommendations.

The two-hour copyediting test required me to edit three articles (two short and one longer piece) and write one press release using AP Style. The only thing I knew about AP style going in to that exam was AP style does not use the Oxford comma. I was given a laptop and an AP style manual. I spent at least an hour on the first article, looking up every single point that I suspected was there to test my editorial eye and AP style knowledge. An hour into the test, I realized I had to finish. I stopped after I edited the second article and quickly wrote up the press release. I then edited the longer piece, which I had been asked to cut at least 250 words from and write a title and cut lines for. I finished with ten minutes to spare. I turned in my work, and I was asked how I felt about the time constraints. I was honest: "I think I would have been at least thirty minutes to an hour faster if I were more familiar with AP style guidelines. If you hire me, I'll buy a copy and start working on learning the rules right away!"

As I packed up to leave, my cello in the corner of the room, I knew that if I wasn't invited to a second interview or extended the job that it would be because there was a candidate with better AP style knowledge.

Some interviews are about the devil you know. Familiarity helps. I was showing an interest in the university by playing in the orchestra. One professor commented casually in the hall that the university I was trying to get a job at could be a "pretty insular place. You have to go and knock on doors and get your feet on the pavement." I networked with professors on campus through the music department.

I specifically asked one person who they knew in the department I planned on interviewing with and asked if he could put in a good word for me. I don't know if that's what happened, but asking for help didn't hurt my chances. Also, a good word from someone the hiring committee knows goes a long way. I have personally seen people who were in a "no" pile put into the first interview pile because a mutual friend of the hiring manager asked them to look out for the résumé. Don't let a feeling of pride of "making it on your own" get in the way of your success.

On the job, success was harder to define. Even though I held a doctorate and worked at a university, I was never given the space or opportunity to use my title. Like many other women, I was always introduced by my first name. I didn't get to set the tone for how I wanted to be treated in the office. As the days turned to weeks turned to years, I realized that formalities were most often used when first meeting people. I accepted that I would see my title only on hotel reservations and the occasional wedding invitation.

The World Doesn't End When You're Fired or You Quit

While I've talked about searching for work and interviewing, it's also important to discuss when it's time to quit. I stayed in one job until I was fired. It was a terrible fit. I knew from the first day of training it was the wrong job. But if I quit, my training wouldn't be paid. So I stuck it out until they let me go for "failing to perform to standard." I assure you, the world didn't end when they gave me the heave-ho. I bought concert tickets with my first and only paycheck from them. When you work at a place for less than a month and don't even finish training, you can leave it off your résumé.

Shockingly enough, people quit things all the time. Because I so rarely quit activities, I had a hard time wrapping my head around leaving a job, even when it was a bad fit. As I work more jobs in more places, I have discovered that people walk off after a break and never return. This is a true story. We sat at the break table for lunch and one person got up and never came back.

I had one job that sounded perfect on paper. After a few weeks, I realized it was a terrible fit. Lacking confidence, I had bid too low at a place where I was promised there was room for growth. However, the reality was that the only growth was applying for jobs in other departments as they opened up. I felt deeply unhappy and bored. Every day was the worst day ever. I woke up every morning regretting not having died in my sleep. I would bribe myself with lunch off-site if I arrived on time, just to get myself out of bed. Then I had to drive to work. When I didn't get killed on the way to work, then I had to get through the day. I sat in my car full of dread and nausea. It was not a good time in my life, and I soon started looking for a new place of employment.

What didn't help was that I was going through the worst time of my life. The dog that my partner and I had adopted was dying of leukemia. My engagement with that partner was ending. In all seriousness, I was one more personal tragedy away from starring in my own country song or leaving town on a Greyhound bus. The poor movers had to make sure they were packing up the right things and dividing other things in half as I moved into my own apartment. Then I turned thirty a few weeks later.

I don't know how else to describe the level of bad that year was in my life, but even then, it wasn't as bad as the year I finished my dissertation. I held on to the idea that one day, things would get better. I focused on a proverb used by the Zapatista movement: "They tried to bury us; they didn't know we were seeds." Life was trying to bury me, but I was going to grow from the experience. I was a seed. You are too.

No matter what happened, I was going to make a career change on my own terms. I enlisted the help of a trusted mentor and began to aggressively apply to jobs all over the country. I could have stayed in the job, but I also wanted to sever all ties with the place I had been living. Too many memories were in that state. For me, I knew what city I wanted to end up in. I was willing to do something for a few years that perhaps wasn't the most perfect fit, just so long as I could be anywhere but the city I was in at the time.

As you begin to reevaluate your career and life path, remember you can choose what happens next. If you can't change cities, look at other opportunities in the town or online. I am happy I managed to finish my degree, but I don't really use it all that often. Learning to accept where you are in your life at the moment you are in takes time. Here are some questions to get you started on your transition to a new type of career.

- What are three things in your life that you won't give up?
- What are five jobs other people have said you would be good at?
- What are three reasons behind why a friend, family member, or celebrity is happy with their life?

3

Getting Over the Fear of "No"

There are a thousand pieces of advice I wish I had had when I started graduate school or when I was trying to find my first job, but the thing is I didn't know what kind of tools I needed for my toolbox, and I didn't know I could ask or should ask other people. The most important thing I wish I had known was how being told "no" or failing would not be the end of the world. For many, many years, anything less than an A, less than perfection, was unacceptable.

Many people drawn to academia are deeply perfectionistic. So perfectionistic that they'd rather sabotage their success than risk rejection for their best work. I know. I'm a recovering perfectionist myself. It's a process, and one that's not a done deal yet, but perhaps one day I will be more at peace with my perfectionistic tendencies.

Imposter Syndrome is when someone feels they are a complete fraud and will be exposed at any minute as one, regardless of their accomplishments. Even after success in my field, I still feel like an imposter. There is this creeping sense that someone is going to figure out I'm the equivalent of three wiener dogs in a suit. Like the scene in *The Wizard of Oz* where the curtain is pulled back to reveal the human behind the omnipotent floating head, I always feel as though I am not good enough.

Perfectionism Can Lead to Self-Sabotage

Engaging in self-sabotaging behaviors like setting unrealistic goals and self-expectations is a way to beat yourself up and give in to the feelings of inadequacy that are both real and omnipresent in a scholastic environment. Whatever you do, set reasonable goals for yourself. How? Track your progress and be honest about the progress, even when you fall short of your goals. Compare the original goal to the actual progress. Adjust the goal. Keep goal activity time sacred. Honor yourself. Honor your dreams. Don't cut yourself off at the knees by saying you'll do everything the day before something is due if your actual output will only get you to halfway done.

I used to run on sleep deprivation and self-loathing. Having to recalibrate my career trajectory meant having to be rejected over and over and over. Going to job interview after job interview where the main focus always shifted to, "So, why aren't you teaching?" felt like failure after failure.

Spending nine months on the job market (and all the lovely sexist overtones that amount of time of being unemployed brings) made me realize it was time to get over the fear of people saying "no" to me. I got some good advice: "You only have to hear 'yes' once." By realizing the worst that would happen in the job application and hiring process was that I would be told "no," I learned to be more confident in what I applied for and what I asked for as salary.

The first dream is not the only dream, possibility, or future. If eight-year-old me had had her way, we'd be digging for fossils or rock hounding. Or living on Mars. Or creating a domesticated velociraptor to ride to school. Or being a local journalist. True story—I used to print my own newspaper stories on a dot matrix printer, and the baby birds hatching outside my window were BIG NEWS.

Go Ahead and Plan, but Things Still Go Awry

Life not going to plan is often the first "no" many people experience. There's a popular joke: How do you make God laugh? The answer is to tell God your plans. That is to say, for as much planning and organizing as you do, something won't go right.

Plus, rejection in any form plain sucks. First things aren't going well; then you have to go and change tack. I barely knew what I wanted to do after I graduated. The uncertainty brought me back to the summer when I worked at a baseball stadium. My favorite patron question was, "So, what are *you* doing here?" The implication there was either that something was wrong with me or that I had done something wrong to end up working in food service. While some of my coworkers struggled with drug or alcohol addiction, many more were trapped in a vicious cycle of poverty. They worked two or three jobs, sold their plasma, and had no health insurance or safety net. I left the uncertain hours and lack of benefits behind when the summer ended. Many of the others I worked alongside could not.

Labor is seen by many businesses as an unwarrantably high expense. Wages cut into profits, and in a system that rewards continual profits above all else, labor is the enemy. I used to feel as though the graduate student union wasn't necessary for me. I had a fellowship and then funding via a teaching assistantship. I thought that the union wasn't doing anything helpful to me. I learned how wrong I was when I spoke with friends who attended other schools without unions. Their work hours weren't capped, and they had few to no benefits. I thought my job situation was normal. The same goes for working for companies. What you think is the status quo might not be.

The first step is figuring out what is customary and usual. When I was in graduate school, I learned this by meeting another student from a different campus branch. This student pointed out that our class and teaching load was very high.

There were credits in the catalog to reduce the number of courses you needed to take, but we weren't allowed to use them. What we were told was not the way things were done on other campuses.

Much like with business, the deadliest phrase to progress is "that's how things have always been done." As I started teaching classes, I was told to add students who showed up the first day to a paper waiting list. When the person supervising you says that is what you do, it's hard to question what you're being told. Here's a corollary—just because that's the way things have always been done doesn't mean things are being done right or efficiently.

It's scary to push back. For years I went along with the adding-students-who-showed-up-the-first-day-on-paper system. I didn't think about the fairness of this informal system. It rewarded people who ignored the full class online and still showed up. Another problem was that it created an unfair advantage for students who knew they could ignore the full notice when signing up online. What should have happened was opening up an official, digital waitlist through the online course management system.

Again, I did nothing for years. I sat back and went along with what I had been told to do. One of our colleagues refused to do that anymore. Collectively, we realized that for every five extra students five of us took on, we took away a teaching assistant position from someone else. All we were getting in return was more work and less time for our own studies. Being the first person to stand up is terrifying.

As one ex-partner liked to tell me, "Make sure you prep the battlefield." If you are going to have any kind of confrontation with an authority figure, make sure you prep the battlefield. Behind closed doors, many of your colleagues will grouse and grumble with you, but when you lead the charge up the hill and to the authority figure's door, well, don't be surprised if you look behind you and there is no one there. You need to make sure you have all your documentation and support lined up before you go running into something unprepared.

Also, be very aware that by being the one to put the face and name to whatever complaint or dispute will very likely end up with you facing negative consequences in that department, whether it's not being selected to teach additional summer sections or being unable to work with a certain faculty member ever again. This applies to work situations too. Be prepared that going against a figure of authority in your workplace may mean that you will be looking for a new gig sooner rather than later. It isn't fair, but the world rarely is. Learn when to fight battles and in which battles you are being used as a pawn. Always ask: Whose battle is this? Who benefits? Will someone else step forward to change things?

I learned that lesson the hard way. My friends outside of my graduate department pointed out that we had a larger grading burden compared to other disciplines. We were expected to mark homework, essays and essay corrections, and exams and exam corrections. I would often see the same assignment or test two or three times. The painful truth is that the students who understood the value of revisions did them and the students who didn't made more work for me. Fellow graduate students in the department broke down and cried in their offices over the workload.

Data and proof are great tools. Even though I felt as though the workload was heavily weighted down with administrative things, I didn't know for sure. Drawing on the strength of the colleague who pushed back against the class size increase, I made an appointment to talk with the supervisor about the amount of grading. I did not come into that meeting unprepared. In fact, I had meticulously kept track of my hours and activities for two quarters and had encouraged my colleagues to do the same.

I went into that meeting utterly terrified of being told that, no, nothing would change and that I had placed a target on my back for no reason. What I had, though, was the graduate student union contract and my proof where my workload was the heaviest. I could counter, with evidence, every excuse where I was told I didn't work hard or efficiently. What I held in my hands was proof. Proof of overwork and proof of what activities were taking up the most time. I knew the stress and amount of time things took were not all in my head.

The result of that meeting was a reduction in workload. No more reviewing corrections of corrections. Fewer exams worth more points. The IT department would batch upload files to the online class shell rather than have instructors individually upload files that had been batch emailed in large chains. I faced my first terrifying professional confrontation, and I had made things better for future teaching assistants.

I knew asking for a reduction in activities and number of exams given was worth risking hearing "no." If I didn't ask, then nothing would change, and the workload wouldn't get better. Small "no"s can join together to push back. It's terrifying when you're at the front. In the long run, pushing back can make a world of difference.

Hearing "No" Isn't Easy

How do you begin to confront the fear of "no"? The internet is rife with quotes about papering walls with rejections or how each shut door means one fewer to knock on. It doesn't mean that hearing "no" for your work gets any easier. Rejection is hard to take. I stopped submitting to literary journals because I didn't understand why my work wasn't good enough. After several rejections, I shelved this book project for years. All the criticisms of the original outline were valid—as it stood, the project was too narrow, was too specific, and wouldn't reach a broad audience. I let it sit in the back of a drawer. Then I realized the original, first draft was one way to tell the story, but that what I had actually learned was far more profound. Two proposal revisions and several long nights later, I had a story that answered the original concerns. Even after I found a publisher, I had to make significant revisions several times.

As to the creative work, well, I recovered from my Imposter Syndrome rather quickly when I saw work by MFA classmates that I judged to be weaker than my work getting published. (Oh, yes, I went back to school and got a second master's after I did a PhD.) I made it my goal to find places to get published in. I had a good friend and writing partner who took a decade off from submitting. He lost the wind in his sails after he received rejection after rejection. I had seen his work. I knew it was quality. He had gotten so many "no"s that he didn't have the drive to move forward. I convinced him to let me submit a collaboration we had done a few years before. Rather, I told him he had three days to tell me not to send our stuff in.

One of our pieces I submitted was accepted for the anthology. He was stunned. All the rejections he had gotten were erased in the span of an afternoon. The important lesson here is to build up others. Some see life as working hard at knocking and keeping people down. Instead of dog-piling and adding to the misery, find a way to lift others up. One of the most encouraging conversations I had was with the chair of an Ivy League university who said that my paper topic was interesting and publishable. Her sincerity didn't cost her much—merely a few seconds of encouragement.

Hell, I pitched a book idea to a publisher at a conference. I got a "Yes, give us a sample chapter and outline," which isn't a "no"! If I ever manage to find the time to do the research on the topic, I will have to check if the editor is still with the publisher. If he is, well, then I can say, "Hey, remember when you said 'Send me a chapter'? Well, I'm ready to send you the chapter. Do you still want to see it?" As with job applications, the worst that will happen is the editor or publisher says "no."

So, go to a conference, chat up some agents, book editors, and publishing representatives. See who might be interested in your finished work. At least you'll know which publishers might want you to send sample chapters or a manuscript before you spend the time and effort on a book proposal. You'd be surprised how putting a face to a topic and a manuscript can really warm up the conversation.

When you receive business cards, put a note to yourself on the back of it like, "Met at MLA 2017, gave me free book because I couldn't stay until half priced Sunday." Then, when you write or strike up a conversation with this person in the future, you can put in that anecdote: "I really enjoyed the copy of [book] that you gave me at MLA 2017. We spoke about possibly publishing an edited volume on [topic], and I was hoping you would be interested in pursuing this publishing opportunity." If you need to follow up at a specific time, create a calendar reminder with the email or phone number of the individual. Business cards are a great tool for keeping in touch, especially when you may not have built up the relationship to where you connect digitally.

Setting Yourself Up to Hear "Yes"

If there is something you want, ask nicely for it. I wrote to the Kindle suggestion email, asking if they had plans to add a Spanish-language dictionary, since they offered one in English. I received a reply stating there were not any plans to add a Spanish dictionary, but that they would keep my request in mind for the future. A few updates later, the Kindle team added one. Being able to click on a word and immediately see its definition reduced my reading time, increased my vocabulary, and improved my comprehension. All it took was emailing a question. If there is a service you enjoy using and see something that could make it an even better tool for yourself, there is no harm in asking.

Set reasonable goals. Forgive yourself when you don't reach them. It is very easy to beat yourself up for not being as good/fast/important as someone else in your department/field/life. Imposter Syndrome is very real, and engaging in self-sabotaging behaviors like unrealistic goals and self-expectations is a way to beat yourself up and give in to the feelings of inadequacy that are both real and omnipresent in the academy.

One way to get over the fear of "no" is to do something you're afraid of. Something you put on the back burner. Life only goes forward. Don't wait for the perfect time. Now is perfect enough. If you need permission, you have mine. Go forth. Do not give up. You are worthy of the risks you are about to take and the uncertainty that those challenges will bring.

When you begin to frame conversations and opportunities as "the worst that will happen is they say 'no,'" you begin to make things less about your fears and more about your possibilities. If "no" is the worst that will happen, then it's worth the risk of hearing "no." Besides, if you don't try, you won't have the chance to succeed.

When I first met some of the students who were close to defending their dissertations, I asked them how they managed to get through all the readings every week. "Game face," they answered. This is the academic version of "Fake it until you make it." There will be some weeks you cannot do all the readings, your teaching duties, and everything else in your life. The solution is to put on your game face and act like you have everything done and together. Do not betray any weakness or shortcomings. You can also think of game face as your "poker face." As far as anyone else in the room is concerned, you've got all aces.

Game face works when getting over the fear of "no" as well. Put yourself in the mindset that everything will work out. Sure, things will miss more than they hit. That's life. Risking rejection is one of the most difficult things to do.

Always look for the bright side of the situation. I'm not naturally an optimist. I often turn to the positive, because if I didn't, I would remain cynical and jaded. Cynicism is often a symptom of the numbing grind of graduate school, so find the bright side and be positive, even if it is as simple as "The weekend is in two days."

Approach new opportunities with the attitude that until you hear "no," it's not a completely shut door. This is especially true when trying for sources of outside funding. As a writer, I always look for small grants to make setting aside time to be creative easier. One way to look at applying for funding, competitions, or scholarships is that they often have better odds than the lottery. I assure you, I was buying a ticket when that multistate jackpot got near $1 billion. Instead of gambling with random numbers, you could be one of only a hundred or so applicants. Also, not all funding opportunities require academic affiliation. Some can be used to better your community. Some are provided by your community. Put on your game face and think that a half-a-percent chance of receiving a scholarship is better than a zero from not trying at all.

I have two fellowships I apply to each year. In part, it's because there is no application fee for either one. But a main reason is that I don't think I'm out of the game. I have the skills to be successful, and if I don't apply, the committee won't know I exist. I spend a few hours working on the packets. I use the application process as a way to frame my independent work for the year. If I am selected for a fellowship, that's amazing. If not, then I've created a project and timeline that I can use on my own for the rest of the year. A few hours of my time could pay off in a big way. Risking rejection every time means I also *open myself up to the possibility of success.*

The possibility of success is exciting. That hope and happiness is often lost in the win-lose rhetoric we are surrounded by. Instead of framing the "no" as something negative, look at it as you being brave. You were braver than hundreds or thousands of other people who saw that same opportunity and decided not to try. For one of the fellowships, they tell how many applications they receive each year. I see the number of people who applied and think that being brave and trying to be selected as the finalist is better than looking at the results and wishing I had given it a shot.

I once won a senior picture package in high school because I was the only person to respond to the ad asking for marketing ideas. A win by default is a still a win. How many other people in my high school saw that ad and didn't do anything? Sometimes it's enough to try. Perfection is the enemy of done. I didn't think my ideas were that great, but the company who posted the ad thought they were good enough for a senior photo package. Remember: nothing ventured, nothing gained.

Get Used to Hearing "No"

Once you hear "no" enough, it becomes less scary. One "no" from an organization is not a "no" forever. It means "no" this year. "No" right now. As you and your career grow, so too does the probability that you will hear a "yes." If you give up before even trying, then you've already lost. Put on that game face and go for the "no."

When I mentor students, I make applying for scholarship opportunities easy. I find two opportunities they are eligible for and tell them they must pick one. There is a big confidence boost when someone in a mentoring position says,

"You're qualified for this; let's work on the application to-gether." I am happy to report that one of the students I mentored was selected for a scholarship. I was so proud of her work, and I was happy to have nudged her into completing an application. Remember, if you don't apply, then you can't be selected.

But, you have to balance personal and professional obligations. This is why having a list of three things you won't give up for anyone else is important. Those three things are the lens through which you can frame your priorities. You can't get everything done in a week—rather, you can't get everything done to perfection. Some things will have to be done to good enough. By applying the principle of triage, you can focus your energy on what absolutely needs to get done and what would be nice to get done. I use lists to help prioritize. I start with the most important thing, whether it's a fellowship application or client presentation, and then work my way down to the small things like dishes. I look at what I want to accomplish that hour, that day, that week. Examining the weight and importance of each activity helps determine its position on the list. The concept of triage provides perspective, much like the idea of what is on fire and what needs to be allowed to burn.

The dirty secret behind my to-do list is that I don't check off every item. After a week, I sometimes decide that certain activities are no longer a priority. The same thing happens at work with projects. There are things I was asked to do at the beginning that are no longer priorities for the company.

If you love your research, continue to pursue it. If you pursue in-depth research, then find a publication avenue. If the project isn't strong enough to be a monograph, consider article-length work. Pitch to magazines or newspapers. General audiences are hungry for accessible research. Many publishers will accept nonfiction based on a proposal. I queried several agents and publishers before I found a home for this book. It took five years of asking and trying. Every firm "no" was just one more place I had tried and could cross off the list.

It's important to remember that you have to hear only one "yes." Think of it this way: Why is something you lost in the last place you looked? Because you stop looking once you find it. Getting lucky once erases all the "no"s that came before. How many publishing houses are kicking themselves for passing on J. K. Rowling's first Harry Potter novel?

Putting Yourself Out There and Looking for Work

The same goes for searching for work. It's hard to put yourself out there application after application. I applied to more than five hundred jobs and got very few interview invitations. At least 120 of those jobs were for faculty or lecturer positions. I had a total of six interviews out of those five hundred applications, followed by four second-interview requests.

As my search became more and more desperate, I wondered if anyone would ever hire me. I had tried to do everything right and perfectly throughout all my studies. I thought maybe there was something wrong with my application materials. Perhaps even something wrong with my skills. I remember wanting to give up entirely. But I was told, "You only have to hear one 'yes.'" While it wasn't easy, I kept going. I was about to give up even looking for work when I got my second interview at my current job.

As you look for work, remember that you are the same fish you always were, but now in a bigger fishbowl. While you might have book knowledge, there will be people who have years or even decades of industry experience. Learn from them. The people you meet in professional contexts are more often than not very happy to help you network. Business is about connections. In a large global marketplace, people choose to do business with companies they like.

You can plan your way out of any situation. Job you hate? Dreams don't have to be grandiose, merely a hope of a better tomorrow. You can find a new gig. All it takes is time. You aren't tied to a bad decision, bad place, or bad job. You make the priorities.

Remembering Your Priorities

I was reminded of the importance of priorities when I finally got my first full-time job. The neighborhood I lived in had a common mailbox. I stopped by after work and found a bubble-wrapped package from my aunt. It wasn't my birthday. Christmas was months away. In the garage, I sat in my car with the engine off and ripped open the top. Inside was a delicate silver necklace. I didn't recognize it.

In her careful handwriting, my aunt explained that the charm was my grandmother's thumbprint. My grandmother had wanted me to receive that necklace when I had finished my PhD. My aunt felt that settling in to my first full-time job was a good time to send it along. She was right. I had finished what I promised my grandmother I would do, and I was starting a new chapter in my life. Oh, that letter made me miss my grandmother. But I knew her hope for me and desire for me to find happiness was in that necklace.

The necklace reminded me that it only took one "yes" to unlock the rest of the possibilities. Although I felt discouraged at times, I worked past the fear of "no." After repeated rejections, I was finally starting toward something new.

Having gone from the darkest months in my life to a fresh start in a new career, I felt a renewed sadness over my grandmother's death and a feeling of joy that she knew I was going to make it through that journey. Holding her thumbprint against my thumb felt like I was holding her hand again.

Here are the next steps to do after reading this chapter.

- Pick one dream goal—a place to get published or the top of your field. Then write out how you would get to that end point.

- Write down why you are afraid of hearing "no." Is it your ego? Is a "no" confirming your worst fears?
- Make a list of three things you want to try for in the next year. Work on concrete steps to make those three things start happening. Remember—the worst thing you will ever hear is "no," and if that's the worst, then it's worth trying for.

4

Is It a Dragon or a Windmill?

The beautiful thing about time is that it's linear. The further along we go, the more perspective we have about what happened in the past. The trials and tribulations of our childhood—not wanting to take a nap, not having the right color socks—are soon miniscule when compared to adult concerns of housing, career, and existential angst. In order to know what situations might be trivial one day and what ones might matter, I have devised a simple question: Is it a dragon or a windmill?

What do I mean by something being a dragon or a windmill? According to Western mythology, dragons are fierce, fire-breathing creatures. Dragons are meant to be slayed. Now, by windmills, I borrow from my literary background, specifically the novel *Don Quixote*. In one scene, the protagonist charges at windmills, telling everyone else that they are giants. Now, if those windmills are truly giants in your world, then go ahead and charge at them. I'd save my charging at large things for slaying dragons.

With that in mind, is what you're about to fight a windmill or a dragon? A life-changing decision such as a career move is a dragon. Work on slaying it. Anything that is not the equivalent of a dragon is not worth your time or emotional energy. Windmills can wait. Dragons cannot, since they breathe fire and all.

Speaking of fires, you will need to learn how to decide which fires to put out and which fires to let burn. There are only so many hours in a day. You can't live your life trying to please everyone else. How do you determine the difference between something you need to handle right away and something you can have wait? As my parents like to lament, the problem with common sense is that it's not that common. I know I heard them tell me more than once that I was "making a mountain out of a molehill." Now, if your yard is infested with moles, then molehills can become mountains. It's all a matter of perspective.

One of the hardest things to gain in life is perspective. Oftentimes that perspective comes long after the fact. To begin framing the situation in your mind, ask yourself the following questions. Will this really matter in five years? Ten? Fifteen? Twenty? You have to balance the overwhelming sense of the moment with the larger picture of the future. The pressure and stress of the moment often makes it seem that what you are doing here and now is the most important thing in the world. On one hand, yes, you want to make sure you are pushing forward and living your best life, but you have to resist tunnel vision and ask yourself, "Will I look back on this in five, ten, fifteen, or twenty years and still feel this thing was as important now as it was back then?"

Think back about the things that stressed you out five years ago. What were the things that made it feel like the sky was falling? Five years later, would they still make the sky fall for you? There are a lot of things that matter in the moment that are long forgotten years later. The more things we experience, the more likely we are to learn how to manage and handle these events. Life after leaving higher education is very similar. At times, the expectations and events will overwhelm you. It's natural; it's a brand new experience you have not adapted to quite yet. When the anxiety, stress, and panic seem overwhelming, take a step back and ask yourself, "Will this really matter in five years?"

Sometimes you have to lie to yourself. Think of Alice in *Through the Looking-Glass*, when the Queen says sometimes she "believed as many as six impossible things before breakfast." Some days are filled with impossible things. You have to say that no matter how stressful and urgent something is right now, it probably won't matter in a few months or a few years. You have to remember that you are most likely looking at a windmill, not a dragon.

Applying This Perspective to Your Work Life

This same balance between dragon versus windmill holds true to your work life, whether you have an employer or clients. A lot of energy can be spent on small and petty things. Don't get into windmill-level quarrels at work. Many people will spend more waking hours with their coworkers than their own families. Don't focus on temporary annoyances.

Instead, work together to slay the daily dragons. Do not waste energy fighting each other. Be there to build others up rather than tear them down. There is more strength to multiple voices working in harmony. Building others up makes the world better. Tearing others down to make yourself feel better doesn't get you very far. You will meet many people who may not have the same formal training as you, but that doesn't mean their knowledge is any less profound or useful.

You can make excuses, or you can make it happen. Take your pick. Priorities can shift over time, and what was once a dragon is now, in hindsight, a windmill. No matter what happens, move forward with slaying. Think of each end result as a series of steps, like a game board. Most folks don't write a novel overnight. Breaking apart tasks into smaller chunks takes practice. Start out by keeping track of how long it takes you to do the task—coffee and internet breaks included.

Note when you are most productive. For me, I am most focused and energetic with personal projects at night. Determine if you are intrinsically or extrinsically motivated. Intrinsic motivation means you do the action for yourself and would do so regardless. Extrinsic motivation means you require a reward or want to avoid punishment by doing something. Find out what kind of learner or researcher you are. I am extrinsically motivated. I need to see a carrot and stick from someone else. Otherwise I don't care. I am not good at self-motivation.

As you move through the mental game board of each task, have a goal for reaching that space on time. The reward doesn't have to cost money. It can be as simple as watching an extra episode of your favorite show. At the same time, you can't set goals so far out of reach that you never complete them. This is often a common habit of perfectionistic people. What often happens in those situations is that people will put things off and procrastinate until there is a general sense of panic. Thus, if things don't go well, the blame can go on the lack of time rather than the work itself being inadequate. Another characteristic of a perfectionistic personality is that the work becomes a representation of the self. Any criticism of the work becomes a criticism of the person.

There's nothing wrong with a strong work ethic. I know a lot of my success has come from working longer and harder than my peers who were smarter and better in my field. I wasn't the smartest person in the room, but I was one of the more curious ones. However, the problem is that many employers know how to use that personality trait of working until it's perfect until you are chewed up and spit out. A lot of them will hide behind "well, you're salaried" as an excuse to push you to work all sorts of hours.

If the goals are never achievable, then this begins a cycle of self-sabotage. When I was working on my dissertation, my counselor helped me realize I was engaged in this circle of procrastination, panic, and reaction. I began to rework how I approached projects. After I better got a handle on breaking projects down into manageable parts, I was better able to recognize that same pattern in others.

Perfectionism Is the Enemy of Finishing Things

I worked for one boss who always put things off until the last minute. I was once given fifteen minutes to review sixty pages before the document was presented to the client. The person who created the document wasn't the most attentive to details. It was riddled with errors, from misspelled client name to incorrect punctuation. When the boss handed the project to me to fix and review before the client saw it, there wasn't much I could do. However, he was such a perfection-ist that he didn't look at the presentation until right before we were supposed to present it to the client. Conscious or not, it was a form of sabotage. The original proposal writer was known to produce sloppy work. To have it dumped in my lap with no real time to make corrections revealed more about my boss's poor time management skills than my ability to perform my job.

Why do people put important projects off until the very last minute? In part, it is so that when things don't go well, it can be blamed on outside forces such as not enough time rather than the work not being adequate. Thus, when we didn't get the new business from the poorly supervised proposal, it was someone else's fault—mine for not catching all the errors. It didn't matter that the timeline for me to review that size of document was impossible.

Prioritizing my own health and well-being has created a space where I no longer let the poor project management of others impact my daily life. For example, the bid was not going to be won or lost by the fifteen minutes I had to review and correct typos. Those decisions were made long before that packet crossed my desk. Editing a page every fifteen seconds is not conducive to a successful project bid. One doesn't have to be a mathematical genius to figure that out. I didn't take it personally when we lost the bid.

By knowing how long activities such as writing, editing, and data analysis take, I am better equipped to push back against unreasonable deadlines and manage expectations of what can be accomplished. Rather than running at top speed all the time, I have learned to step back, reflect, and move decisively rather than quickly.

When you are used to working multiple deadlines from various people, you get used to juggling projects. Sometimes that juggling can become rapid cycling. If you aren't careful, you will burn yourself out. How this played out for me was that I can work very hard for a very long time, but I can't sustain weeks or months at a breakneck level. At one point, I had the equivalent of three full-time job duties on my plate. I realized after almost a year that either one of the jobs had to go or I was going to go. I was working at an intensity that was negatively impacting my emotional, mental, and physical health. I could no longer sustain the demands on me. I moved into a role that was much better defined and I reported to a new manager. Both changes made it possible for me to no longer feel like my position was overwhelming. I learned how to do my best work without engaging in self-sabotage.

Another benefit to understanding how I best work is that I can be gentler with myself. The cycle of procrastination is vicious. It's seductive to think, "Oh, I still have time." Better project management skills has meant removing the pressure and panic of a looming deadline. Now, I find working on personal and side projects much more manageable when I don't set myself up for failure. When I take on clients, I look at what they want and how long it will take me to achieve what they ask for. I no longer create impossible situations for myself. Well, I no longer intentionally do so. I recognize how I am extrinsically motivated by outside deadlines. I'll create things here and there for myself, but to finish a project requires me to have an outside goal or motivation.

When I have time-sensitive personal projects, I excuse myself from social functions early to work on them, if necessary. I manage my calendar in such a way that I am not scrambling. Of course, that was not always how I operated. When I started my dissertation, I didn't know where to start. Everything was a dragon. I remember feeling completely out of my depth. I sat and stared at the blinking cursor for hours on end. I waited until the words could come out perfectly onto the screen, but they never did. By the time I realized I was so far behind, I had no other choice but to spend another year working on the project.

My Biggest Dragon Was Finishing My Thesis

My dissertation was the dragon. I had to slay it. I spent my last year in absentia, meaning that I was doing research outside the state and not on campus. The next year of my life was writing 250 words a day an hour at a time. Every day, I walked the dog and then sat on the couch. While the puppy napped, I aimed for the word count first, then the time limit. If an hour elapsed and I hadn't reached the word count, I stopped. If I reached the word count before the time limit and was having a difficult writing session, then I stopped.

After months of chipping away word by word (and one writing session where I typed obscenities over and over again along with "cow goes moo cat says meow" like something out of The Shining), I had a breakthrough day. I managed to write ten thousand words in one go. An entire chapter flowed onto the page. Writing felt electric that day. All the citations and ideas melded together. I haven't experienced a creative day like that since. At the time, all the daily practice and discipline of small, attainable goals gave me the structure to have that successful experience.

There were plenty of unsuccessful experiences, starting with the two years I spent reading and writing my first dissertation chapter. But I also added to my own misery. Now, this may come across as common sense that should have been common for me, but don't move during your dissertation year, if at all possible. I moved across the country twice the year I finished my dissertation because I like to live on hard mode, apparently.

Even with the wonderful ten-thousand-word session, I wasn't done with my dissertation by the time I moved again. In my ideal world—before I got better at managing my own expectations of myself and project managing my writing output—I planned on being in the revision and editing stage by the time I had packed for the Georgia-to-Texas move. I ended up writing my last chapter in various hotels and motels with a dog, two guinea pigs, and a partner. I frantically finished up my last chapter while at a friend's house after I had driven back to California from Texas to meet with my adviser. His comment that my final chapter was "a little rough" was an understatement, but I got that chapter done and approved, and then I defended my full dissertation to my committee.

As I entered the home stretch of my dissertation, I kept in mind my father's advice, "The enemy of good is better." I also kept in mind that the best dissertation is a done dissertation. The time to be picky is not when you haven't finished what you are working on.

When my adviser planned his summer research trip that year, he thought, "Do I have any students graduating?" He had concluded that, no, he didn't have any students graduating that year. In his defense, I had one finished chapter and was in the middle of my second chapter six months before I wanted to defend a completed dissertation. I don't know how I managed to finish the rest of my dissertation on time, but I don't blame him for not thinking I would graduate in June. My adviser was amazing at getting chapters back to me with feedback; however, if you had asked either of us in December if I was going to be able to graduate in June, well, let's say that my photo finish to graduate impressed even myself.

In the end, the dissertation was about the process of learning how to write a longer and more involved thesis and project, not about being my magnum opus. My dad recently read through it and pointed out that a few paragraphs stopped randomly in the middle of sentences. I tried to blame the uploading and printing process, but I'm pretty sure I just forgot to finish what I was saying.

The process of professionalization and categorization continues to be pushed earlier and earlier. Because youthful success is celebrated early, often, and loudly, it is easy to feel like your work should be more, or have happened sooner, or that you are not worthy of what you are striving for. From gifted classes in elementary school to taking graduate coursework while still an undergrad, American students are pushed to be more extraordinary, more brilliant, more driven than previous generations. When your advisers admit they would have never gotten their jobs if held to current job marketing standards, it's hard to accept that you did everything you could and still didn't make it. I ended up second-guessing everything I'd done, and I found it hard to forgive myself for the choices I made. Part of me felt like a failure for not having a debut novel by the time I finished high school, which is silly.

Recovering from Perfectionism

I call myself a recovering perfectionist because getting down on myself for goals and dreams I haven't accomplished is really easy. I work hard at harnessing my energy and drive into new endeavors without letting my desire to be immediately perfect get in the way.

Good is good enough for your term paper/thesis/dissertation/client presentation. Your goal is to finish your degree or show something to a potential customer. Living in hyperperfection is destructive. The point to use that discerning energy is when something is meant to be final and published for public consumption. Mistakes and errors can always be fixed before something is finalized. However, you have to have something that is ready for that sort of scrutiny. Sometimes you have to say a thing over and over until you believe it, but I promise, the enemy of good is better. When we try to make something better, we often make the situation worse.

What I took away from the dissertation process was a different perspective of priorities and long-term goals. Looking at the parts that make up the whole process made the final document less intimidating. I would set goals of researching and pulling three articles every other day and reading at least one. Because I didn't have regular access to a university-level library, I learned to plan my research time very judiciously. During my research trip at the Library of Congress, I had a solid list of books to request and read. I had cross-referenced which ones were not available anywhere else in the country or held at libraries too far away to access. Every time I visited the nearby university libraries, I made sure to arrive as early as possible so I could read and take notes for the most time. These focused, research-heavy days provided the foundation for the writing days that followed.

On particularly difficult writing days, I would type up quotes and ideas I planned to use. I knew I wouldn't use them in full, but I let the words count for my daily goal. When I had good writing days I would shape, rework, and engage with the quotes. Those also were the days when I would delete a lot of excess or extra words. However, after several months of writing my dissertation a paragraph at a time, I had begun to make real progress. The first chapter I wrote that I had agonized over was a blip on the radar. Each subsequent chapter was easier and easier to write. In part, this was due to the constant expansion of my knowledge base. The more I knew about the topic, the faster and clearer the ideas came to me. Sometimes that meant stepping away from the computer and writing on paper.

In a digital-heavy world, it's easy to forget that drafting by hand is a very valuable tool. I relied on writing on the computer first because of my procrastination habit (that I have not completely broken myself of, by the way). Putting something off until the last minute meant that the first and last draft was usually the same document. Try as I might, that same tactic did not work for the chapter I needed to write to sit for my doctoral exams. Oh hubris and hindsight. I learned to work to smaller, more manageable goals. I also learned to focus on specific, daily tasks to accomplish those goals.

When things feel overwhelming, focus on writing down lists of what you need to get done. Start with what you need to accomplish by a week. Then focus on what needs to be finished by a day. Finally, focus on what needs to be done in the next hour. By breaking things into smaller chunks of time and smaller goals, you are working to slay the dragons and not get distracted by windmills. The reason I advocate writing down these lists is twofold: First, it gets the stress out of your head and onto paper. Second, you can see how much you accomplish and if you need to readjust the expectations and goals you are setting for yourself.

Learn to say "no." Learn to say "no" and mean it. Learn to get out of things tactfully and gracefully. Learn some polite brush-offs like, "Thank you for thinking of me. I'm flattered but I can't do that right now." If you want to help, but you don't want the full responsibility, turn the question back to the requester. Put the onus of "no" back on them by offering a solution or compromise that you're willing to do. For example, you could tell them, "That sounds like fun. I don't have time to sit on the planning committee this year, but I could hand out programs the day of the event." This turns your offer back on the other person. They now have to refuse your offer of help. It's a preemptive compromise. If you don't have time or energy for something, it's perfectly fine not to participate.

This does not apply if you are "volun-told" rather than asked to volunteer. If you are volun-told, well, don't put any more effort into the project than you have time for.

Anything that interferes with, impedes, stalls, or derails your major goal is not your priority or responsibility! A committee that will take time away from your research? Offer to help on the day of the event. You are not personally responsible for the success or failure of someone else's projects. Another person will step up if you decide you do not have the time or emotional energy to participate or run/organize/plan something. If not, well, then it's still not your problem or guilt trip.

The Perspective My Dissertation Gave Me

Perspective and crisis shape us. We learn how to evaluate dragon versus windmill. You get to be selfish when facing dragons. You can tell other people "no" if what they want takes you away from accomplishing your goal. I assure you, if something is important enough to a group, they will find someone else to do what they are asking you. Or they'll find a way to make things happen without filling the position.

From my own personal crises, I found that the best way to defeat dragons is to learn from your prior encounters. I don't know what it is, but my luck is such that I have had three computers fail on me without warning. Twice during finals week. I now keep a cloud backup and print hard copies of major projects as a precaution. Technology is my dragon, but I have learned how to make a data loss a minor annoyance rather than a personal catastrophe.

Channel your energy into moving forward. You can't live your life in reverse. However, you do get to grieve. Grief is a process. One day, you might look back at those hopes and dreams with nostalgia instead of regret or loss. It is one path not taken. For some careers, yes, it is difficult to go back to.

Is the door to me being a professor closed and locked? That depends on how you look at things. I chose not to be an adjunct instructor. At times, I am tempted to go back to academia and teach. To say that I'm completely over leaving the tenure-track job hunt would be a lie. I still feel jealous of colleagues who got the dream jobs they wanted. But I also feel happy for their successes. In particular, it's weird seeing school supplies when you're no longer in school. For many in the working world, August and September are just months on the calendar. When I see those sales, I have to confront the grief all over again.

Take time for yourself. Don't beat yourself up. You have to accept where you are in the moment. Moving into a new direction takes time, and it takes a lot of reassessment to be able to move forward. But you have to move forward. You cannot allow yourself to be frozen by perfection. Agonizing over every little detail is counterproductive. Keep going. Don't stop. Don't apologize.

The good news is that the perspective of time helps lessen the rejection of the past. When so much of your self-worth is wrapped up in a professional identity, it's easy to get into catastrophic thinking that this was your one and only chance or that you'll never be happy again. You can always try for something again. What you end up doing might not perfectly fit the idea you had in mind when you started out. We have a culture that celebrates youth and untested talent. It means we are expected to burn hot and fast. Very few people can sustain a working tempo that takes all their waking hours and waking energy. You are more than your job.

Sure, there are people younger than you with more professional success, more money, more whatever. There are people older than you with more of that as well. You have to live your own life. A lot of us follow our parents' advice and end up living their unfulfilled wishes or trying for careers that inoculate against their worst fears. Even so, a professional job doesn't mean you will never get laid off or that you will never experience a toxic workplace. A job is a series of activities you do in a building. It's not the end all, be all.

I'm not asking you to create a masterwork overnight. You have to keep going forward. And onward. What you're doing doesn't have to be perfect. It only has to be finished. Rarely are we finishing something entirely on our own. There is a review process to most things. Even clothing has a numbered inspector.

Facing new obstacles and challenges means having a mindset of understanding that one day this crisis won't necessarily be a crisis in hindsight. Sometimes you are going to have to tell yourself, "At least it's not as bad as that." Sometimes you will have to lie to yourself. If what you're experiencing is the worst that you've ever had to deal with, then tell yourself that one day this will be funny. Say, "This will be a funny story one day," over and over until it's plausible. Even if the story won't be funny, you'll have a story to tell. Worst case scenario, you are finding out what the lowest point of your life is. Then, during future crises, you have a bottom you (hopefully) won't go below.

How Do You Handle and Get Out of Your Lowest Point?

Lie to yourself on repeat. I'm not kidding. Sometimes the best way to handle a terrible situation is to say that things will get better. Know that if this is the worst you have to go through, then you're learning what rock bottom is. My rock bottom was the year when my dog died, my engagement ended, half my furniture broke in a cross-country move, my guinea pig died, and then my grandfather died of lung cancer the day before my birthday.

Unlike when my grandmother had died while I was in school, the series of bad events didn't set me as far back emotionally. I had better priorities and stronger boundaries between my professional and personal identities. How I handled difficult event after difficult event was not perfect, but I was not falling apart. I had gained critical perspective of what was important in life. I wasn't going to bring myself down putting energy into windmills.

Tell yourself that going forward, you will have a new benchmark for bad. I certainly do. It takes a lot for me to have a bad day, week, month, or year. I have a new perspective on awful. When comparing new, stressful situations to that rock bottom, not many events are truly dragons. A lot more are windmills. If there is no way the situation will ever be funny, then at least you will know that you can get through the next crisis.

After Attempting to Star in My Own Country Song, I Left Texas

I want to share how life after leaving Texas went. I had quit a state job from which I could have retired and gotten a pension, working in a role that I will call Devil Wears Prada meets Portland Plaid.

The first day, I hit the ground running—ordering lunch for a business meeting the boss had forgotten about, refilling coffees, and generally trying to figure out what my role was going to be.

The second day, well, that's when things got interesting. In his office with the door closed, he laid out his expectations for the position and what I should be doing on a day-to-day basis. Then he thought for a moment, leaned back in his chair, and said, "I want you to anticipate my needs."

There isn't a good answer to that. I held still and hoped that things stayed in the noncreepy category of work life.

"I have some meat chickens," he began. Pursing his lips and leaning back in the Herman Miller Aeron chair, he contemplated a few moments. "I want you to kill some chickens."

For once in my life, I decided this situation was not going to be made better by talking. I kept my mouth shut and let him continue.

"I need you to kill them for me. There's four, and I don't care how you get it done. Maybe you can find someone on Craigslist."

Yes, I was asked to kill chickens for my boss on my second day of work. I asked friends how to best butcher chickens. Those friends told me the word I was looking for was slaughter. I watched videos online to be able to do it humanely. I exchanged emails with someone who stopped replying when I asked about price. I found a place in another town where you could drop the chickens off by 8:00 A.M.

and have them ready by dinner. But the boss didn't want to pay mileage or for any potential car cleanup (which I knew to ask for because I had worked a state job that had guidelines and rules for travels and work times). The boss got cold feet about my solution when I offered to bring a date who I had met online to do the dirty work. And what a third date that would have been. To be clear, I have not killed any chickens.

Fun note—my willingness to problem solve this request meant it became a job interview question. Literally. After I made a lateral move within the company, I told the second replacement this story. She said, "Oh. That's why he asked if I'd kill chickens for him during the interview."

Other challenges that appeared in that position that were not quite dragons revolved around airport drop-offs and pickups. The first time I was going to drive the boss to the airport in his car, my date asked if I could drive stick. The answer is no. I can't drive a manual car. The date asked what my plan was if the boss's car wasn't automatic. I said, "Wake you up and take you with me." Fortunately, I didn't have to do any gear shifting. There wasn't any point in getting worked up over whether or not I could drive the boss's car until I got in for the first time.

However, there was one small incident with the boss's car. He always insisted on driving to the airport, and then I would drive the car back. One trip was very early, and it was the boss and another employee flying out. He parked the car right in front of a speed bump. I did a head check and started pulling forward. I heard this awful, metal-crunching noise. I looked again and kept going forward. The noise got worse.

I realized what was happening.

I was not having some strange trouble with the speed bump. I was hitting the mini metal stop signs they have marking the crosswalks at the drop-off area. Halfway over the speed bump, I had to go forward. I'm certain if I put the car into reverse that I would have ripped something out. There was no way to fix the situation but to continue to traverse the speed bump.

The screeching of metal got worse. I couldn't pull over to look. Not if I wanted to make it back to work without crying.

"It's probably not that bad," I said. In the parking lot, I got out and looked around to see the extent of the damage. Fortunately, there wasn't even a scratch to the clear coat.

I got back to the office and checked my phone. No message from the boss. For almost a week, I had hope that he hadn't seen my mistake.

As we coordinated pickup times, the boss texted, "Please avoid the small stop signs when you pick us up." Busted. So much for getting away with that mistake unnoticed. Apparently he turned to the other employee and said, "Remind me to check the car when we get back."

But it wasn't worth getting upset over. Spending a week stewing or worrying over what the boss would think was a windmill. There were far more important things to focus on. Perhaps if that had happened at my very first job, I might have panicked more. Whether it's youthful heartbreak over not having someone ask you to slow dance in middle school or ending a long-term relationship later in life, time provides distance and perspective. Upon reflection, many dragons are truly windmills. Don't go tilting after them. Go forward. Go onward. Don't pour unnecessary energy into the things that won't matter in five, ten, twenty years.

So, how do you start putting things into perspective? Take a look at the list of questions below and look outward at the situation and then inward toward yourself.

- Today's dragon is tomorrow's windmill in hindsight. How can you use each crisis as a way to gain perspective on the difference?
- Focus on the most important things—you are not your job and the job you are working now may not be the job you have in five years. How can you not let unimportant things get in the way of the big picture?
- Sometimes moving forward means lying to yourself. Either this will be funny one day, or you'll have a new benchmark for bad. But tell yourself tomorrow will be better, even if you don't believe what you're saying.

5

Chasing Chickens (and Other Shit I Didn't Think I'd Have to Do with a PhD)

A few months after being asked to slaughter some of the boss's chickens, those descendants of dinosaurs came back into my life. In fact, it was New Year's Eve. I had made plans in advance—as many folks who work as assistants are wont to do in their own lives—and my boss had changed his the week prior. Like the organized-event-and-outcome person I am, I moved all my personal life chess pieces around to accommodate the shift.

The morning started with a text message saying he wouldn't arrive until 7:30 A.M. because he didn't feel he needed to be at the airport that early. At five in the morning, I did the math to see if this change in itinerary would prevent me from making my later morning obligations with my friends. The margin of error shifted from two hours to thirty minutes. It wasn't ideal, and things would be tight, but the round-trip was still doable.

Already awake and unable to fall back asleep, I sighed and killed time on my phone. When the boss rolled up to my apartment, he said we were going to stop by a local coffee drive-through place before going to the airport. I knew something was up the instant he offered to buy me a coffee too. In all the early morning runs, even the first one where my date asked if I could drive stick, not once did that man offer to buy me a coffee. He inevitably had his own vessel of piping hot liquid, but I, the mere executive assistant, wasn't worthy of a token of appreciation for working extra-long hours.

When people behave outside their usual manner, it's best to arch your eyebrow. It didn't take a doctorate to figure out something was up.

If you need to know what life as an executive assistant is like, imagine watching a toddler with two fistfuls of glitter—then pretend that most days you get the glue away. What follows is not one of the glueless days.

On the way down the hill, the conversation indicated that it seemed like something had gone wrong at the office and that I would need to fix whatever had gone awry. As my duties included managing client follow-up and outgoing communications, I wanted to get to the bottom of the issue as soon as possible. After I'd ordered a polite-sized medium chai latte, the boss dropped the bombshell. He had left the office too late the night before to get feed for his chickens. For those of you lacking grandmothers who paid for college with a prize-winning 4-H heifer, the reason chickens need a constant source of food is that if they run out of food, they will turn to cannibalism. Yes. That's right. If left to their own devices, these domesticated fowl will rip each other apart with their beaks. They also have a particular penchant for ripping out cloacas. It's such a problem that there are chicken eyeglasses. Yes. Chicken. Eyeglasses.

My boss told me I needed to go to his house after dropping him off at the airport to feed his chickens. I wish that were some kind of euphemism. I frantically texted my date. (Yes, the date who offered to help slaughter chickens. It had been going well. The dating. Not the slaughtering of livestock.) No matter what I did, I was going to be late. My entire plan revolved on going straight to my date and then going out for New Year's Eve. No extra time had been planned for an unexpected chicken run.

Because the only plans I had to return home were to grab my car and go off on the rest of my weekend, I was caught completely off guard. The boss didn't live nearby from where I lived and where work was located. There also was no way I could come back in the evening without missing the plans I made downtown with my friends from out of town. There was no good solution that didn't let someone else in my life down. The least bad option was to be late to my date who was upset that, once again, I was putting work responsibilities first.

I drove out to the boss's place. Traffic wasn't bad. I pulled up and quickly unloaded the large bag of chicken feed. Things were going well. In fact, as I finished placing the rest of the chicken feed in the large feed bin, I looked at my watch and saw I might still be able to make it to the original start time for the date. I felt a rush of relief as I closed and locked the gate.

Nothing Is Ever as Easy as It Seems

What happened next was straight out of a movie. I heard the chickens cooing. The sound brought back memories of my childhood running around my grandmother's farm in rural Kansas. However, I quickly realized that the clucking noise was on the wrong side of the fence.

With the same trepidation of the person who opens a door in a horror film, I looked down. A beautiful black and red Croad Langshan was to my left.

This is the point in the story, gentle reader, where I must pause and explain that there were not one or two chickens in this coop. Oh no. I need to clarify that there were at least thirty. Thirty birds who spent their days roosting and waiting for freedom. Opening the gate and shooing the escapee back in was not an option. Not when twenty-nine other chickens pressed against the gate in anticipation, hoping to join their comrade.

Then the situation got worse. My boss had an outdoor cat. I saw that kitty's tail in the tall grass alongside the garage. The serpentine flick and rustling betrayed the crouched predator.

"This isn't good," I thought.

Then the chicken took off. For those unfamiliar with barnyard fowl, let me enlighten you to a few things. One, chickens can and do fly for short distances. Two, chickens are fast. Three, chickens are mean.

The problem wasn't that this silky feathered creature was hop-flying away from me. The problem was that it was hop-flying away from me toward a several-acre expanse of open field, which was then compounded by the cat going into full hunter mode.

And, no. No, this was not one of the chickens slated for execution my second day of work. That would be too easy.

I asked myself, "How do you catch a chicken?" My mind raced through all my childhood memories. I had watched my uncle put a chicken to sleep, but I didn't remember how he'd caught the chicken in the first place.

The next thirty minutes were spent alternating between screaming either "Bad kitty!" or "Here chick chick chick" while trying to coax the bird closer to the gate by keeping my arms open wide and running around like a toddler pretending to be an airplane. All with a cat stalking and trying to pounce on the fleeing fowl.

Each lap around the coop, I thought (with some colorful language rhyming with "duck" sprinkled in between),

"What did I do to deserve this? Where did I go wrong in my life? I have a PhD. This was not the plan. Why am I chasing a chicken when I have a PhD?"

Finally, the other chickens wandered back inside the coop, and I was able to leave the gate open long enough to chase the loose chicken back inside.

Because I had spent so much time at the farm, I didn't have time to drop off the car at work and walk home like every other time I had taken the boss to the airport. Instead, I had to shuffle my car out of my parking spot and leave the boss's car in its stead. I saw my landlord in the window and pointed at my car, then the boss's luxury black car. She nodded and gave me a thumbs-up; she understood that she shouldn't tow the car above my pay grade in my parking spot.

That evening, while I hung out with my out-of-town friends, the boss sent a group text to half the employees because his neighbor said a black car had been parked in front of the boss's house for an inordinate amount of time that morning. He specifically asked if I knew anything about that. I looked at my phone, weighed the consequences, and replied, "No idea, do you need me to go check tomorrow?"

Turns out that another employee had stopped by for some equipment. Also turns out the boss forgot to lock up the house before he left.

Everything was quiet and fine, until a few days later when I had to drive back home in a snowstorm. Even though I told my boss where his car was parked, he didn't have his wife drop him off to drive it home when they got back to town.

I couldn't move the boss's car as the snow poured down in buckets of white fluff, nor was I going to try and maneuver it down the steep hill. Grumpily, I parked my car on the street and hoped it wouldn't get taken out by a snowplow or neighbor.

All I wanted was to get that car out of my parking spot. It took an extra day or two for the snow to melt, then it took me and another coworker to do a proper vehicle shuffle between work, farm, and my house.

Then my boss's wife learned that he had asked me to feed the chickens. To say that she was not pleased would merely start the conversation. She was utterly mortified that her husband had requested I go feed their chickens. She swore I would never have to do anything with the chickens again. I didn't even have to fess up to the escaped chicken, which was nice.

Sometimes It's Okay to Lie

The lesson? Sometimes it's okay to lie to your boss or omit details of how things went. Especially when he made you feed his chickens on a Saturday. Even though he bought bribery coffee. If I had to do that day over again, I would have gotten a large chai latte with a few extra shots of espresso. There was no point in politeness when being bribed.

Spending a morning chasing chickens also brought back some of the regret about my life choices—not in a facetious way either. Had my life gone so wrong that I was living above a garage and working a job that was not where I saw myself at thirty? This was not the plan. Seriously, who has "chase chickens" in any part of their life plan?

Sometimes Life Doesn't Go to Plan

Grief will hit you at unexpected times. Jealousy as well. Both are valid emotions, considering the years you poured into something that didn't happen. Other people might have the life you thought you wanted for yourself. It's harder to swallow that fact when you perceive that they didn't work as hard as you did and still got what you wanted.

This brings me to the touchy subject of money and debt. In the United States over the past several years, many changes at the government level have made this level of education something where the student bears most of the risk. With the elimination of subsidized graduate loans and talk about taxing tuition waivers the same as income, the risk of career change through education is falling squarely on individuals rather than employers or the government.

With that in mind, if you decide to do a career change that requires a new (or another) degree, you need to ask yourself if the debt you are getting into is something you can pay off. If possible, limit the amount of student loan debt you take on to no more than the average annual salary for the job you think you'll work after leaving academia—or even working in academia. You may not make as much money as you think you will. Some tenure-track jobs I applied to offered only $28,000 to $30,000 per year.

I had friends who were in the doctoral program with me who made more in the jobs they held prior to quitting to attend graduate school. It was a nasty shock for all of us when we realized our doctoral degrees were not going to unlock this magically high salary. Some people get lucky: one colleague was hired by a very renowned university with a starting salary of $80,000 and a $10,000-a-year research budget, plus relocation expenses. The salaries in the field are shrinking along with the available positions, along with job security.

With so few jobs paying six figures or more right after graduation, it doesn't make sense to go into multifigured debt for a career that doesn't match that number. I've contemplated a career change to teaching K–12, but the state where I live now requires a master's in education in order to do so. I'm not keen on spending another year's potential salary on a new career pathway.

The problem with how the conversation about education as panacea is set up is that we make education the only path to professionalization. We also push people to pursue education in fields where they have little to no practical experience. People buy into professions based on prestige and perceived return on investment.

I have always been bookish. One of my peers commented, "You were always busy reading. Always." I loved *Star Wars* and science fiction before it was cool. Being a lifelong nerd meant that I always envisioned professional school as part of my plan. At first, I thought I would enjoy law school and being a lawyer. After two internships, I realized that I was no longer certain about that as my pathway. Eternally practical, I knew that law school was a lot of debt to go into for a job that I wasn't 100 percent certain about.

I was vaguely aware that employment followed education. Lots of ink had been spilled over graduate English degrees being useless in an overcrowded field. Instead, I leaned toward Spanish literature. When I started considering graduate school, the US economy had not yet collapsed, and the foreign-language job market had approximately a one to one ratio when it came to graduates and jobs. I had started teaching and tutoring as an undergraduate, and the teaching bug had bitten me pretty hard. Chasing chickens around a rural farm was not what I envisioned I would be doing.

Having to capture an escaped chicken while doing a job that doesn't necessarily require your doctoral training gives you time to think. One loose chicken is an annoyance. Thirty loose chickens are a problem. Pick chasing a single chicken rather than trying to round up thirty. When you leave the academy, you will encounter people who are unkind to you because you aren't teaching. You will have to learn how to tell your story about leaving the academic job market without sounding bitter. And maybe, just maybe, you'll end up chasing some chickens while you figure all that out.

- What's your chicken chasing story?
- Is there something happening in your life right now that could possibly be funny with the benefit of hindsight?
- You don't have to figure everything out right away. But how can you work on chasing one chicken instead of thirty?

6

The Best-Laid Plans of Mice and Control Groups

No matter what you do, even your best-laid plans will go awry. There won't be parking outside the place where your job interview is happening. Traffic might be at a standstill. You might not know what you're supposed to be doing on the first day of your new, nonacademic job. Chickens get loose. That's okay. It doesn't matter if it could get worse or better, what matters is that you have the knowledge, skills, and training to make your plans come to fruition.

A lot of people like academia because at first blush, it seems to be a set way to have a career and focus in life. The formula is sold as school plus degree equals job. The actual journey is not so straightforward.

My father reminded me of his favorite medical school joke: "What do you call the person who graduates dead last in medical school? Do you know the special name they give that person? Doctor." The same was true for me when I finished my doctorate. It didn't matter that I finished my dissertation with less than twenty-four hours to submit it to the university to graduate the year I did. My photo finish is nowhere in the official paperwork. All you see is that I got it done.

With no idea where to turn or what to do next, I remember the best piece of advice I heard during graduate school: How do you eat an elephant? One bite at a time.

Anything—grading, homework, dissertation, thesis, or work project—can seem impossible or overwhelming. It can feel as though you are being asked to swallow the entire elephant in one single bite. One solution is to step back and evaluate the process and steps necessary to complete the task. The best way I found was to actually time and measure how long certain tasks took me to complete. Projects require time and research.

Find your rhythm. Work at times when working is best for you. I am, and probably always will be, a bit of a night owl. My favorite time to write is at night and most often after 5:00 P.M. It's a habit I got into when I was in K–12 because I would go to school, do after-school activities, then come home and start on homework. I often don't even get into a writing frame of mind until after I eat dinner. I know this is part of my rhythm, so I plan my writing sessions accordingly. For a while during the dissertation-writing process, I worked until the early morning, sleeping on the couch and moving back to the bed after my partner had left for work.

I made lots of online friends in England and Australia because of my odd schedule.

Time management is essential to your personal and professional success and sanity. You have to decide what kind of schedule you want to have. I like having my Friday nights completely free of work or freelance obligations. When I was in California, I didn't do anything related to school after 5:00 P.M. on Fridays. By having an evening completely off and away from school, I was able to take a break. I use that same philosophy when I use vacation time. I log out of all work email and often leave my phone behind or off the entire trip.

I had one colleague who refused to do anything related to schoolwork on the weekends. She got up at 5:00 A.M. every weekday to accomplish this. Another colleague made sure to devote her entire Sunday to her family and church. What all three of us had in common was that we made priorities. We also scheduled our activities in advance. My personal time-management technique is something I call "blocking." I divide my days into fifteen-minute blocks. I then conceptualize or write down every single activity I need to do. I also set a goal time to complete those tasks. You will be surprised how many fifteen-minute chunks of time you will find in your day.

Sketch out how many blocks of time a task will take you. Along with setting and creating reasonable goals, keep accurate track of how long certain tasks take you to do. This is helpful for an office job as well. I know and keep track of how long different tasks take me. That way, I can push back against unreasonable expectations or demands of my time. It also helps you keep your projects on track and on time. On my best days, I can get about a thousand words written an hour, but that is only for projects that are nearly complete or that have extensive research behind them. Otherwise, my best is around 250 words. Knowing that, I am better able to plan my writing time and know what reasonable results look like. Rather than promising to write an entire novel in a weekend, I know it will take me a couple of weeks.

Even with this blocking method, you have to plan for the unexpected. Power outages. Urgent projects. Things outside of your control. You have to give yourself some fudge room. If you push yourself to the wire, you will wear yourself out on a regular basis. Sure, I can up my writing production or pull a lot of late nights, but that's not how I want to work all the time.

What about Life after Academia?

Make the brand of you. You must highlight your skills and assets for your future employer or client. Reassure them about what your unique skill set will bring to them. There are people outside of your academic world. Translate your knowledge into their language.

Find ways to make sure what you are doing furthers your long-term goals. Go broad and work down to the narrow. If your dream is to publish a cookbook, then make it a goal to try and create one new recipe a week. When I was still doing coursework, I worked out an arrangement with a professor to be able to explore topics for my dissertation in my final class essay. By doing that in two separate classes, I finished most of the research and writing for my first dissertation chapter as part of my regular coursework. This saved a lot of time and had the added bonus of getting feedback from a faculty member who was not sitting on my committee.

You are not your job. You are not your job title. Even if you are very good at your job, you are still more than the position you are filling. I am all for taking full professional pride in what you do, but I also know that the jobs we hold today might not exist in twenty years. There is most likely a job out there that I will end up doing that doesn't exist today.

As you start to figure out what the next steps in life should be, learn who is a voice of reason and authority. Listen to their advice, then weigh opinions and evidence. Some advice will be dated, and some advice will helpful. Not everything will pertain to your situation.

Also be sure to use your network. Networking is how you will find work inside or outside of academia. With many jobs never advertised, it is important to make connections with professionals in your chosen or future field. It goes back to the "devil you know" versus the unknown. A recommendation from someone who works in that company can take a résumé that was passed over and get it a second look. If you are looking for work while currently employed, be discreet. Otherwise, make sure everyone knows you are on the job search.

Read message boards. There are flyers being pinned up on message boards all the time in coffee shops and outside libraries and being taped to store windows. Take a quick look to see what they say. Sometimes you will find interesting opportunities being tacked up in a hideous shade of neon. Sign up for job alerts. Dust off your professional online presence so employers can check you out.

Sometimes What You Find Is Too Good to Be True

Sometimes opportunities are too good to be true. Or rather, they don't turn out how you thought they might. During my foray into alternate academic work, I spent a lot of time online. One website I enjoyed and frequented posted a unique job opportunity.

I took my own advice, got over the fear of "no," and sent off the materials the internet company asked for. The company liked what I had sent in and what I proposed to do in their marketing department. They wanted to interview me over the phone. I was so excited. The position looked like a dream job with amazing potential for personal and professional growth.

Thanks to that phone interview, I learned that sexism was still alive and well in 2013. I also learned the hard way that you need to watch what you say and how you say it. During the phone interview, the CEO of the company asked me what I liked to do on the weekends. I answered, "I like to read, watch some shows on my Roku, play Guild Wars 2, and we take the dog for a walk most evenings."

The fatal word was "we." A properly trained interviewer would know better than to ask the questions I received next.

"Who is we?" he asked.

My inner monologue was a litany of obscenities. There was no good way about it. I mean, if it was illegal to ask someone if he or she was an axe murderer, and you were directly asked if you were an axe murderer, there is no good way to answer it. If you refuse to answer it, because the question itself is illegal, you look like an axe murderer for refusing to answer the question.

My only choice was to answer the increasingly aggressive and personal questions from the CEO. The CEO also appeared to express an open contempt for my doctorate. I hadn't thought the interview had gone well, at all. I was shocked when the CEO contacted me to set up an interview with the person who would be my immediate supervisor. This phone interview went much better, and I directly asked this person if holding a doctorate would be a problem. The individual responded that he began doing start-up work with people who held doctorates, so he recognized the value of my skills and degrees. Since this person interviewing me would be my immediate supervisor, I agreed to go out of pocket for the cost to come up to interview at their company and be reimbursed after the interview was over.

Everything in the city where the company was located was sold out because of a huge convention. I drove to save the "strapped spinoff company" money on a flight. I ended up renting a room in an attic because there were no hotels within sixty miles of the city where the interview was happening.

The in-person interview went fine, until the CEO once again began asking inappropriate personal questions such as, "Will your partner be moving up here with you?" and "Well, how do you think you'll fit in here, I mean, you with your fancy PhD. Both [future supervisor] and I dropped out of college." It was such an antagonistic and hostile interview. I went through the interview in kind of a haze of anxiety and anger.

I was shocked when the CEO offered me the position at the end of the day. Having recently experienced a bait-and-switch situation where verbal promises were not honored or backed by written contracts, I insisted several items be included in the offer of employment, such as moving expenses. The pay was lower than I wanted to accept, so I also tried to negotiate for a higher starting salary because I had researched what the average salary range was for the job duties I was being hired for, and the salary I was being offered was lower than industry average in that city.

Now, the reason why I won't name the company, despite the fact that they deserve to be shamed for how they treated me during and after the interview process, is that it is a fairly large company. I have evidence of the job process. However, all the illegal questions were done verbally, so it's my word against theirs. Because this company gave me a written offer, they could not hire anyone else in that position unless they proved the person they made a new offer to was more qualified than I. Well, having a doctorate and speaking four languages makes it pretty hard to meet that legal standard of proof.

Oh, the company hired someone else to essentially do exactly what they were asking for that position name I applied to, but again, they couldn't use the job title they offered to me, because I never refused the position, and, in fact, maintained that I wanted to be employed in the position even after the offer was retracted.

Also, even though the parent company is very large, the actual branch I interviewed with is a small entity with fewer than fourteen employees, which means I couldn't file an Equal Employment Opportunity (EEO) complaint. Believe me, I looked.

What made me angriest about the entire experience was not the illegal questions or the retracted offer, but the fact that this company used the ideas on their website that they solicited from me during the interview. I received no payment nor any attribution. At the end of the day, I was asked what kind of blog post I would write for their contracted campaign that was ending in a few weeks. I said exactly what kind of blog post I would write and how I would incorporate certain elements. Well, a few weeks later, my blog post idea was up on their website. I'm glad I drove up for the interview and got fleeced for ideas—no, really. It taught me a valuable lesson: plagiarism and thieves are everywhere, and you have to protect your intellectual property and ideas.

When I later recounted how I had been duped and used to a local businessman, he told me what I should have done. I should have said, sure, let me borrow a computer so I can send you an email with my ideas. Email equals paper trail. Paper trail means proof of theft. I stopped being able to even log into the site I had been a part of, because it wounded me emotionally to see the ideas and suggestions I had made during the interview appear on their website, and know I had no chance of any restitution. I had said it all out loud, and I doubt the other people in the company who witnessed both the illegal job questions and how my ideas were incorporated without attribution or payment would find it in their collective conscience to corroborate my account.

Handling Job Interview Questions

You may receive interview questions that I like to call "fishing expeditions." The questions in and of themselves are not illegal; however, they are posed in such a way you may accidentally or unthinkingly disclose information that has no place in the job interview.

The most common "fishing expedition" question I received was, "So, what are you doing here in [this town]?"

Looking at my résumé, nothing tied me to the state I was living in. Having gone through several interviews prior, I knew how to turn the fishing expedition into my advantage. This is why you should take interviews even if you're not 100 percent sold on the company. Interviewing is a skill that requires practice.

In the interview, I told the truth: my parents used to live in the town over, and I really liked the area and wanted to come back after I graduated. It was a version of the truth. Did my interviewers need to know the whole truth about my relationship being the reason I moved there? Absolutely not. I didn't wear my engagement ring either. I also made sure I reworked my speech pattern to say "I" and never say "we" when talking about weekends or activities or interests. Anecdotally, any interview I wore my engagement ring to did not result in a callback. All interviews where I left it off resulted in subsequent interviews. Hooray sexism.

Use interviews as a time to see if the company (or client) is a good fit for you. Ask hard questions like the turnover rate and opportunities for advancement. Look at employee desks. Are there personal effects and photos or is everything stripped bare? If a place is going on and on about how they offer free coffee and there's not much else, well, that's not always a great sign.

Along with that, keep in mind that you don't have to take the first job offered to you. Even if the offer hadn't been pulled at the internet company, I still had a bad feeling about working there. The fact that my interview consisted of the

CEO bragging about the annual open-bar boozefest where everyone got plastered did not make me feel safe. Given the abusive line of questioning I endured during the interview, I'm not surprised that Silicon Valley's nickname is Sexist Valley.

Trust that gut feeling. If a job feels off, it won't get better over time.

No matter what you do, you can plan as much as you want, but life won't necessarily cooperate. Be prepared for things to go wrong. Take things in stride. You are not your job title. You are more than the work you do.

- What are three to five of the most common interview questions for the job you want?
- Have a friend help you practice answering interview questions.
- Research the average salary range in the area and job title you are interested in.

7

Sticking the Landing

This brings me to the title of this chapter, which comes from an image of my childhood of Kerri Strug sticking her vault landing with a severely sprained ankle during the 1996 Summer Olympics. I watched it unfold on live television. Despite great pain, she nailed her landing. Now, she had to be carried to the podium because she couldn't walk on her ankle any longer, but she stuck the landing when it mattered most.

Life is very similar. You have to stick the landing, even if that landing does not include your dream job, or even the degree you started to pursue. You may not even be in the best mental, physical, or spiritual space in your life as you're coming in for that landing, but you still have to stick it. Nail the landing, then collapse afterward.

My Landing Wasn't Great

With that in mind, never minimize how someone else is feeling. When I was in my first year of graduate school, I had a fellowship. This meant that I did not have to teach. I felt fairly stressed out because I had three graduate courses and one undergraduate course, in addition to being far away from my family. However, I perceived that I did not have the space or permission of my peers to complain or talk about those feelings because I "had a scholarship" and "didn't have to do anything like them" at the end of the quarter. I felt the professors had higher expectations of my work precisely because I was not teaching my first year.

The sexist rebukes I overheard, or that the rumor mill circulated, echoed in my head. ("I don't know why we bother giving fellowships to girls. All they do is have babies instead of careers.") There were whispers that my fellowship should have been awarded to another student because some students felt I didn't deserve it.

You will run into folks who feel you don't deserve to be where you are. You also will run into folks who can't imagine you being or doing anything other than what you are doing. Don't let those who are not your champions make you feel inferior. Conversely, don't let those who champion you make you act superior.

Maybe Your Landing Can Be Different

You are loved. This is very important to remember when your life is in transition. There are people in your life who love you. There are friends in your life who will support you. It is easy to let the temporary disappointment of life not going the way it was supposed to get you down.

Never trust the word of mouth about someone else's expectations. I was told my adviser never lets someone defend a dissertation with fewer than fifty pages per chapter, or a total of 250 pages. I defended a dissertation that was around 220 pages. Fortunately, another graduate student wrote a dissertation that was more than eight hundred pages, so by the time I was the absolute last person to defend a dissertation that year, every single professor on doctoral committees was very, very happy my dissertation was short and sweet. However, if I had believed the rumor mill instead of speaking with my committee chair, I would have pulled out my hair and felt like I had to produce more content than was actually necessary.

You have to stick the landing, no matter how much it might hurt when you do.

"How?" you might ask. It's about all the knowledge and training that brought you to the moment where you need to make it count. Do three job-search-related things a week, then work your way up to doing three job-related things a day. Keep doing things in small chunks. I promise, once you get in the habit of breaking down the job hunt into smaller pieces and aiming for reasonable targets (seriously, three things might start with putting on clean underwear—I don't judge), the process of searching and interviewing becomes much easier.

The little bits of advice I wish I had known when I was making major life transitions don't matter. What does matter is that I chose my priorities differently after losing my paternal grandmother. Because I put myself first, I was able to spend time with my maternal grandfather as he died from lung cancer. Despite a year that was, at first glance, much more stressful with breakups, pets dying, moving, siblings' weddings, and then my grandfather dying, I was much better able to handle the changes. I knew who I was and what I was doing with my life. Things weren't perfect, but I knew that in time, everything would be okay, that the bigger picture was greater than the moments that were temporarily overwhelming.

The purpose of life is to stand back up when life shoves you down. Life is going to hit you hard, and for some of you reading this right now, life has taken swing after swing at you. When you get knocked down, get back up. If you get yourself back up, your responsibility is to help those in your life to remember that they too are loved and can get back up after major setbacks.

A small cup of kindness goes a very long way. I leave you with the following that doesn't take chasing chickens around to figure out: be good, be kind, be gentle. Be good to the world. Be kind to others. Being kind does not make you a pushover. Kindness and empathy are wonderful traits. Lastly, be gentle with yourself. If you don't know what three things to focus on to move forward, then start with goodness, kindness, and gentleness. The rest will follow.